RICH BROTT

5 *Simple Keys to*

Financial Freedom

*Change Your
Life Forever!*

Published by

ABC Book Publishing

AbcBookPublishing.com
Printed in U.S.A.

5 Simple Keys to Financial Freedom
Change Your Life Forever!

All scripture quotations, unless otherwise indicated, are taken from the *Holy Bible, New International Version*®. *NIV*®. Copyright © 1973, 1978, 1984 by International Bible Society. Used by permission of Zondervan Publishing House. All rights reserved.

Other Versions used are:

AMP- Amplified Bible.

Amer. Std.-American Standard Version, 1901.

KJV-King James Version. Authorized King James Version.

NASB-Scripture taken from the *New American Standard Bible*, ©1960, 1962, 1963, 1968, 1971, 1972, 1973, 1975, 1977 by The Lockman Foundation. Used by permission.

Scripture taken from the *New King James Version*. Copyright © 1979, 1980, 1982 by Thomas Nelson, Inc. Publishers. Used by permission. All rights reserved.

Verses marked (*TLB*) are taken from *The Living Bible* © 1971. Used by permission of Tyndale House Publishers, Inc., Wheaton, IL 60189. All rights reserved.

Scripture taken from *THE MESSAGE: The Bible in Contemporary Language* © 2002 by Eugene H. Peterson. All rights reserved.

This publication is designed to provide interesting reading material and general information with regard to the subject matter covered. It is printed, distributed and sold with the understanding that neither the publisher nor the author is engaged in rendering religious, family, legal, accounting, business, investing, financial, credit, debt or other professional advice. If any such advice is required, the services of a competent professional person should be sought. In summary, the content contained herein is not given as advice, rather it is strictly for the purpose of your reading entertainment.

Every effort has been made to supply complete and accurate information. However, neither the publisher nor the author assumes any responsibility for its use, nor for any infringements of patents or other rights of third parties that would result.

First Edition, March 29, 2007
Richard A. Brott
All Rights Reserved

ABOUT THE AUTHOR

Rich Brott holds a Bachelor of Science degree in Business and Economics and a Master of Business Administration.

Rich has served in an executive position of some very successful businesses. He has functioned on the board of directors for churches, businesses, and charities and served on a college advisory board.

He has authored over twenty books including:

- *5 Simple Keys to Financial Freedom*
- *10 Life-Changing Attitudes That Will Make You a Financial Success*
- *15 Biblical Responsibilities Leading to Financial Wisdom*
- *30 Biblical Principles for Managing Your Money*
- *35 Keys to Financial Independence*
- *A Biblical Perspective On Tithing & Giving*
- *Basic Principles for Maximizing Your Personal Cash Flow*
- *Basic Principles of Conservative Investing*
- *Biblical Principles for Becoming Debt Free*
- *Biblical Principles for Building a Successful Business*
- *Biblical Principles for Financial Success – Student Workbook*
- *Biblical Principles for Financial Success – Teacher Workbook*
- *Biblical Principles for Personal Evangelism (out of print)*
- *Biblical Principles for Releasing Financial Provision*
- *Biblical Principles for Staying Out of Debt*
- *Biblical Principles for Success in Personal Finance*
- *Biblical Principles That Create Success Through Productivity*
- *Business, Occupations, Professions & Vocations in the Bible*
- *Family Finance Handbook*
- *Family Finance Student Workbook*
- *Family Finance Teacher Workbook*
- *Public Relations for the Local Church (out of print)*

Rich and his wife Karen have been married for 35 years. He resides in Portland, Oregon, with his wife, three children, son-in-law and granddaughter.

DEDICATION

This book is dedicated to my beautiful granddaughter, Ella Faith White. As our first grand child, she has added much joy and happiness to our lives. The 5 simple, but profound keys outlined within these pages will work for her starting at any age. The sooner she understands these principles, the better her life will be. Grandfather loves you Ella!

TABLE OF CONTENTS

INTRODUCTION

It is my conviction that you could sum up the financial wisdom of the ages and condense it within five simple values. They are listed as keys throughout this short, yet timely book.

Here they are:

Key 1   Stop Spending on Yourself
Key 2   Control Your Cash
Key 3   Live Below Your Means
Key 4   Save for Your Future
Key 5   Give to Others

No doubt there could be hundreds of sub-titles under these keys, yet the main principles are effective and to the point. Learn these basics successfully and you will be well on your way to living a life of financial freedom.

To Changing Your Life Forever!
Rich Brott

Key One

STOP SPENDING ON YOURSELF

*M*any people have never learned the art of "living below their means"—essentially, controlling their spending. Spending money to get the most out of it is something you will have to work at, just as you will work to earn it in the first place.

Do you put first things first when you make purchases? Do you buy what you need most or what you want? Do you shop in more than one store to compare the price and quality of a particular item you want? Do you resist the temptation to buy something because it is on sale or just because it appeals to you at the moment, when there are other things you need more?

Let me be very forthright and direct with you. You already have enough. Stop buying more things! You don't need everything. You don't need the latest, the greatest, the biggest, or the best.

Quit watching television commercials. Stop listening to those who are trying their best to convince you that you just have to buy their product. After all, it will help you live a more fulfilled and satisfied life, will keep you in better health, and make everyone else want to be your friend. They don't care a flip about your well being; they just want your money, or your credit card.

KEEP AN EYE ON YOUR SPENDING!

Tune in to what you are spending! Write it down. Don't make it a guessing game. Most people do not even know how to tell whether they can afford something. Everyone, not just those who feel they are short of money, should use a ledger detailing all cash flow.

Virtually every business uses a system to define the inflow and outgo of their cash and so can you. No matter how much money you think you have, it's a useful exercise to determine where it comes from and where it all should go.

Now I want to get right in your face and say this. Living below your means *is* possible. It is just a matter of making different choices; right decisions.

How much is enough? How many things are sufficient? Specifically, just how much money do you need to spend on yourself and just how many things do you need to live in this world? How many possessions must you accumulate to feed your appetite for having it all?

Are you happy only when you indulge your every whim to spend more money on yourself, or can you actually be happy curbing your craving for more and more. Is it possible to place self-imposed limits on your current lifestyle and restrict your personal spending? Are you spending your cash for need or greed?

Use a daily journal to list out-of-pocket expenses down to the penny or nickel. It feels odd at first, but quickly becomes a habit. In the journal, label a page for each category of expenses and record every outlay under the appropriate category. This means every purchase of clothing, groceries, furniture or bark mulch; each dinner out; gasoline, oil and other auto expenses; haircuts and dry cleaning; books, records and tapes; stamps, magazine subscriptions and newspapers; baby-sitting; daily commuting expenses; and so on.

Everybody needs some kind of system to account for their spending and cash flow. Spending needs to be controlled. But first you'll have to find that missing money—the income that somehow flies out of your grasp. Ultimately, it's not what you earn that gives you financial security, but what you save. Many are still trying to learn how to live within their means instead of living above their means. Yet to save more money and spend it wisely, you must first know where your money goes. And that means keeping records.

You may think the records you already keep are evidence enough. Check stubs, receipts and charge account statements do paint the big picture of your rent or mortgage, utilities, car payments, furniture and other major purchases. But the clues you really need are smaller. What about all your pocket money? How were those $50 withdrawals from automated teller machines spent? And the $45 department store charges? What do these sums tell you about your spending patterns?

If you're like many people today, you don't know because you don't accurately keep track of spending. Yet doing so is surprisingly easy. With that accomplished, you'll be able to analyze your spending patterns, solve the case of your missing money and draw up a realistic form for accounting for the missing money.

Once you've discovered how much you have coming in, you get to decide what to spend it on. That's the key phrase: you decide. You are controlling the money, not the other way around. Start by determining how much to sock away in savings and what to pay against your credit-card debt. Then allocate leftover cash for everything else. By laying out your budget this way, you'll see opportunities to cut spending you may not have noticed before.

For example, maybe you'll find you can save $30 a month by eating out less, $50 by buying fewer clothes, $20 by carpooling and $25 by sharing a babysitter. Add these up and you'll have an extra $1,500 by the start of the new year. Invest that money — conservatively, no less — and you'll have more than $20,000 in 10 years. All thanks to some simple cutbacks.

Here are two areas to watch carefully. First, some people find it particularly hard to stick to a budget when they're addicted to credit cards. That kind of plastic is too free, flexible and — ultimately — expensive. So try to kick that habit and switch to debit cards instead. Second, it's crucial to build some free money into your budget each month — even if it's just a few dollars. That way, if there's a CD you have to have or a night you feel like going out with the girls (or guys), you can do it without feeling like a failure.

Once you see how you have been spending your money, set up a workable plan for changing your spending patterns and habits, if necessary, to accomplish your new long, medium and short-range goals.

Keeping Good Spending Records

You needn't pull the journal out of pocket or purse every half hour. Take a few minutes each evening to write down the day's expenses while they're still fresh in your mind. Receipts can help jog your memory, but remember to separate the expenses into their proper categories. The supermarket receipt, for example, may reflect, not only groceries, but also lawn chairs, medicine and other items.

At the end of the month, sit down with your daily journal and checkbook. First, total the outlays for each category in your journal. Then allocate each check you've written into one or more categories, using credit card statements and receipts as reminders. Finally, combine the journal and checkbook numbers and record the month's total spending by category in your ledger.

Remember, a $100 check to Visa tells you nothing. Break it down into $62 for children's clothing, $17 for yard supplies and $21 for a gift. If you keep your daily journal in good order, recording total monthly expenses should take just half an hour or so.

You now have an accurate picture of one month's spending. It's early yet for analysis, but if outgo exceeded income, zero in on discretionary spending such as clothing, entertainment, gifts and purchases for the home. What can you cut down on next month?

Now repeat the process. One month's records tell you little about spending patterns over time. To gain a full understanding of your spending patterns, you need a long-term perspective. Three months is good. Six months is better. Over and above fixed expenses and some fairly steady variable expenses, your outlays will fluctuate, perhaps widely, from month to month.

There are seasonal expenses like vacation, Christmas, birthdays and anniversaries. Some fixed expenses are spaced over long intervals—insurance premiums, taxes and car-registration fees, to name a few. Then come unexpected expenses, such as big medical bills, car repairs and new appliances. All are as much a part of your overall spending profile as groceries, utilities and mortgage payments.

TRACKING MINOR EXPENSES

Keeping track of those nickels and dimes turns casual spending into a conscious, ordered process by linking the act of spending money with the act of recording the outlay. Now instead of thinking about each purchase only once, you think about it twice. This simple exercise builds discipline with your money.

After three to six months of recording monthly expenses, your ledger page will become a spreadsheet, which is a mathematical model of your finances over time. You can follow rows across the page to see how particular categories vary over time. You can calculate average amounts for variable expenses—in effect turning them into fixed expenses, which are much easier to use for planning.

RESISTANCE BUILDING

Just as the daily discipline of exercise, training and hard work successful athletes must practice, so you must approach your desire to stop spending money on yourself.

When you find your spending is out of control and you cannot resist buying more things for yourself, building up your resistance to impulse buying is a discipline you need immediately.

Often it simply comes down to this: saying "no" and have the steadfastness to keep yourself out of temptation's path.

The traits of godly people are characterized by the spiritual disciplines to which they submit. Whether it be prayer, purity, integrity, humility, diligence, faithfulness and obedience or selflessness, leadership, servanthood, and financial stewardship. These are all important.

Economic disciplines include time management, wise spending, hard work, financial stewardship and debt restraint. What is the key to achieving success in all these areas? The key to success is that of personal discipline.

It's a lot easier to tell others how to budget than it is to discipline yourself! Recognize that it's easy to stumble, to make a wrong choice and fall flat on your face in regards to personal discipline. But don't make that your last chapter! Get up, start over, get some discipline into your life and get back on track! There is always hope if you don't give up. So don't give up!

Don't block your path to financial freedom! Stop spending on yourself!

Key Two

CONTROL YOUR CASH

*L*et's get serious about disciplining your cash attitude. The bottom line is this: when you pay with cash, you will buy less. You will pay less. You will want less. The professionals are quick to point out that consumers purchase one third less when paying with cash.

The flip side is that when you use credit for purchases, you may buy more than you could possibly need or use, pay more for the item, and pay more interest. When you overspend, you not only pay much more, but you also severely retard your ability to save and invest.

All the places that are trying to sell you everything from cars to furniture to plasma TV's, also entice you to sign on the dotted line by offering so-called "free financing," 90 days same as cash, interest-free credit, no payments until…etc. Often if you will open an account, they promise a gift. Of course, we've all heard the saying, "there is no free lunch." And so true it is. Nothing in life is free. It all costs you something. You will pay for everything, and sometimes very dearly.

When you are about to be enticed by these sales clerks, TV marketing or newspaper advertisements, pause and think it through. Ask yourself what is the real cost of the item if you purchased it via a credit account. Is it really something you need, or just buying on impulse?

Exactly why do you want this item? Just how much and how long will you really use it. If you think that you need it, stop and think; *if you had not gone shopping today, would you have even been considering it right now?*

If you truly do need it, is this the best price? If this store is able to offer "interest free" credit, will the next store discount it if you pay cash? Can you afford this purchase? Does it make good money sense?

What will happen if you cannot repay the loan? Will making this purchase bring you closer to your financial goals? Is this really such a good deal? If it all seems too good to be true, then perhaps it is.

What are the advantages of paying cash?

Consider the following list:

➤ You will be less inclined to think you really need the item.

➤ You will delay your purchase as long as possible to preserve your cash.

➤ You won't be the impulse buyer you would be when using credit.

➤ You will always attempt to purchase at a discount to use less of your cash.

➤ You won't have to worry about destroying your planned budget.

➤ You won't have to worry about making payments.

➤ You will choose your purchases more carefully.

➤ You will not purchase your wants before your needs.

➤ You will be at peace and the purchase will seem more satisfying when you pay with cash.

➤ You will take better care of your purchase when you pay with cash.

Some of you may try to excuse yourself and think cash could be dangerous to use for it could be stolen. Yes, perhaps that is true, but using a debit card, which is drawn against your bank account that has the cash, is safe indeed.

A debit card, has the same purchase safeguards as any credit card. When using a debit card, the amount of the purchase is automatically deducted from your checking account as if you had written a check.

Think about it. If you paid cash for an automobile, would you buy a brand new one with all of the extra bells and whistles, or would you be more inclined to purchase a great used model? It's a good feeling to use cash to make major purchases.

I don't remember when I last purchased a vehicle on credit. It has been too many years ago. Yes, it does keep me from trading vehicles every year, but who needs to drive the biggest and the best all the time? Only those whose egos need to be maintained.

I purchased all four of my vehicles with cash. Because of it I don't have a lot of cash, but they were all purchased new without credit. In our family we have a boat, a pickup, an SUV and a family van. Because we all work in different areas of the city, it makes having three separate vehicles a necessity. If the city bus came near our neighborhood, we wouldn't need all three.

It is a great feeling to pay with cash. I was born in the 1950s. Back then, 33% of all vehicles were purchased with cash. My first five cars were purchased with cash. All five were purchased during my high school and college days.

I was raised with the attitude that you did not buy something unless you could afford it. You certainly could not afford it unless you could pay in full before taking a purchase home. If you didn't have the money, you saved for it first. It is much better to fund your dreams instead of servicing your debt.

How do you stop adding to your debt load? You simply begin to pay cash for all purchases. If you do not have the cash, you walk away. Using common sense is the best way to stay out of debt. Have the common sense to stop buying on credit and start paying with cash. If you want to freeze the level of your debt, you simply freeze spending.

I took a cyberspace trip to Bankrate.com, used the online calculators and developed the following calculations. If you have credit card debt of just $5,000 at an interest rate of 18%, and make a minimum payment of 2% of the unpaid balance, it will take you more than 46 years to pay it off. During that time, the $5,000 purchase will cost you an additional $13,931.13 in interest. If you took on this debt at age 19, you will have it paid just in time for retirement at age 65. This makes your purchase cost a total of $18,931.13. I hope it was worth it!

As if that doesn't hurt enough, another cost is involved here. It is the opportunity cost of what those minimum payments invested at a mere 12% would have brought to you. Divide the total cost of your purchase ($18,931) by the 553 months it took to pay it in full, and you have an average monthly cost of $34.24.

Investing that monthly for the same time period in a tax-free account would earn you at least $933,682. So it's quite simple. The choice is yours. Do you want to purchase something at age 19 for $5,000, make the minimum payment and have it paid for at retirement? Or would you rather skip that important credit card purchase and have a cool million at retirement with the very same monthly investment?

Making Minimum Payments of 2%		Making Monthly Investments
$34.24		$34.24
Total Purchase Cost	$18,931	$0
Total Investment	$0	$18,931
Money at Age 65	$0	$933,682

These simple statistics will be a wake-up call for many. Time can be a curse or a blessing. Which will it be for you?

No Co-Signing

One huge area of financial vulnerability is co-signing someone else's loan. Co-signing is essentially a quick way to go into debt. People who co-sign feel that they are doing a relative or friend a favor. The potential cost of their signature is usually not explained very carefully to them. When you co-sign a note, you are taking on someone else's debt. Rarely do you know just how much and what kind of debt that person may have. Debt is an excess of liabilities over assets.

A home, if financed conservatively, may usually be sold for more than is owed by the mortgagor. A car, furniture and almost all other depreciating items purchased on time cannot usually be sold for sufficient money to pay off the lender. This is often the kind of debt for which co-signers are asked to be involved.

There is always the possibility that what you co-sign for could be repossessed, leaving you still on the hook for most of the outstanding loan. Ask any credit union or bank how they come out financially when goods are repossessed. Repossession is usually a financial disaster for both the borrower and the lender.

In a given situation, the co-signer may feel some embarrassment at quizzing the lender about what will happen if his relative or friend does not pay as he has promised.

UNDERSTANDING CO-SIGNING

What are you doing if you co-sign a note? You need to understand the financial transaction in which you would involve yourself. Here are three factors:

1. **You are borrowing the money.** The lender has refused to make the loan to the person for whom you are co-signing, based on facts which reveal that the risk is too great to loan the money to your friend or relative.

There is always someone willing to separate you from your money!

When you sign the note, the money is really being loaned to you. The reason you have been asked to sign is that your collateral, your character, your credit and your capacity are sufficient for the loan officer to feel good about the security on the loan. Your signature is the loaner's security.

2. **You are loaning the money.** You are loaning the money you borrowed to a person who was too great a risk for the professional lender. You are involving yourself in a business transaction that the expert money manager would not touch.

3. **You are hoping your friend will pay back the loan.** There's a good chance that it will not happen. When your friend or relative defaults, then you have the privilege of paying back the money. Never co-sign a note unless you can afford to give the money away!

GUARD YOURSELF FROM IDENTITY THEFT

When it comes to vulnerability, nothing is worse than someone trying to steal your identity. Someone who gets their hands on your credit card number and personal information can charge up thousands of dollars in goods and services — and all in your name! If you want to protect yourself from credit thieves, you should start by protecting your personal information.

It seems like everywhere you go, clerks are asking for information—your social security number, your phone number and address, your date of birth, your mother's maiden name, etc. And in most cases, you probably offer this information freely. Yet, this is all it would take for an unscrupulous person to open a credit account in your name or to access your existing account(s) and charge you into financial oblivion.

Here are some strategies to make sure that the only one who uses your credit cards is you:

➡ Don't give out your Social Security number unnecessarily. (Only brokerages, banks and employers are required by law to take your Social Security number.) In case you're robbed, never carry your Social Security card in your wallet.

➡ Be mindful of dumpster divers. Destroy documents that have your information on them before tossing them in the trash. Shred or tear up any pre-approved credit offers you get in the mail, even if you don't respond to the offers.

➡ Demand that your credit company stop selling your personal information to credit card marketers. Stop unwittingly giving your information away yourself, which happens every time you fill out sweepstakes entries and marketing surveys.

➡ Contact the three big credit bureaus (information accessible on-line) and ask them to put a fraud alert on your file. This means a credit company will be required to telephone you before opening up any new accounts.

GET-RICH-QUICK SCHEMES = GET–POOR-QUICK REALITIES

A lot of get-rich-quick schemes prey upon unsuspecting investors. As the old proverb goes, the man who speculates is soon back to where he began—with nothing. This becomes a very serious problem, for all his or her hard work has been for nothing. It is all swept away. He or she is under a cloud — gloomy, discouraged, frustrated and angry. Get-rich schemes rarely ever pan out. That is wishful thinking. Yet, millions of dollars are lost each year to fraudulent deals because of the greed of investors.

The salesperson who pressures you to buy now should trigger a red warning flag in your mind. Consider the friend who drops by to give you an opportunity to invest in a red-hot deal. Unfortunately, you must decide today (they say) because they are going to start drilling for oil in the morning.

Now you may be thinking that you would never be seduced into buying drilling rights over the telephone. Don't be so sure! Greed will get you nowhere. Although many modern consumers have gotten more savvy and are now less easily fooled, greed is still part of human nature. People out there still keep coming up with deals that sound smart to conscientious consumers—but aren't.

Many banks and credit card companies urge their cardholders to buy protection for losses that occur if their cards are lost or stolen and used by someone else for about $25 a year. Many don't know, however, that federal law limits cardholders' liability for unauthorized charges to $50 and then only for charges made before notifying the card issuer. The protection is a waste of money.

Many lenders require borrowers to get credit life or disability insurance. It protects the lender if the borrower dies or becomes disabled before repaying a loan. For the borrower, however, it's no bargain. According to the Wall Street Journal, insurers collect over $2 billion a year in premiums, but pay out only $900 million a year.

If a lender wants you to buy this insurance, explain that your other assets or life insurance will cover the loan if you cannot pay. For example, a term life insurance policy that will pay enough to cover the loan, should you die, is much cheaper. If the lender insists, watch your balance carefully and ask your lender to let you drop the insurance when you've repaid 25 percent of the loan.

EXTENDED WARRANTIES

Many merchants encourage customers to buy extended warranties when they buy autos, appliances or electronic items. They're profitable for the merchants, who pocket up to 40 percent of the amount before sending the rest to the insurer. Don't buy extended warranties on appliances or electronics. While you pay for them in advance, they do not begin until the manufacturer's warranty runs out—up to three years.

These warranties do not cover normal wear and tear or rough handling—the usual reasons repairs are needed. Certainly don't finance an extended warranty. You then pay interest on a contract that won't start for up to three years. Consumers rarely benefit from extended warranties. Name-brand appliances usually don't break down during the first few years and if they do, they're covered by the original warranty. Similarly, defective electronic equipment usually breaks within the first few months and is covered by the original warranty.

Repair Your Credit Schemes

Major credit bureaus offer services that let you check your credit file. Under some programs, you get a copy of your credit file as often as you want for $30-$50 per year and receive notification every time a creditor receives a copy of your file.

Federal law already lets you see your credit file as often as you want and at least one time each year you get a copy of your report free. You may have to pay $10 or $15 each additional time, but few people need to see their file more than once a year.

Being notified whenever a creditor receives a copy of your file normally tells you something you already know—after all, it's your credit, insurance, employment or housing application that triggers a credit request. In the meantime, many services sell the information to direct marketers, who clog your mailbox and call you during the most inconvenient times.

Some companies claim they can fix your credit, qualify you for a loan or get you a credit card. But even legitimate companies can't do anything for you that you can't do yourself. What they will do, however, is charge you between $250 and $2,000. A few credit repair companies have resorted to illegal practices—breaking into credit bureau computers to change a bad credit file, or stealing credit files or Social Security numbers and substituting them for the files of people with poor credit histories. You are better off avoiding them!

Pool Your Debt Schemes

Also called debt consolidation or debt pooling, budget planning or debt adjusting companies, these people end up increasing, not decreasing, your debts, once you pay their debt consolidation charges. Some of these companies charge outrageously high interest or fees that may amount to illegal loan sharking operations. If you need help paying your bills, you're better off visiting a Consumer Credit Counseling office.

Don't pay any company that offers to obtain a Social Security benefits statement, Social Security numbers for your children, or name change when you get married. You can get this information and service free from the Social Security Administration and only you can legally fill out the application forms, so why pay for it?

"Free" Vacations

A favorite giveaway to lure you to sales presentations, such as those peddling condos, is the promise of a dream vacation to Hawaii, the Bahamas or Mexico. In fact, what you get is a vacation certificate. To take advantage of it, you must typically deal with an out-of-state travel agency by mail, not by telephone. It is difficult to get reservations and even harder to get the name of the hotel where you are supposed to stay.

Ask questions, check the answers and consider all the facts before making that purchase or investing those hard-earned dollars.

With many vacation certificates, you must get to the destination on your own, where you will get two or three nights' lodging—probably someplace you wouldn't want to stay. So remember, it's not your education, social status, money or experience that counts. It's taking the time to check it out! If a deal sounds too good to be true, you can bet that it probably is!

"Take-Their-Money" & Disappear Schemes

Most people make major financial expenditures without really looking at all the facts. This kind of action is downright dangerous and certainly not smart. The ultimate cost and alternative possibilities are seldom considered when someone is swept along in a desire to acquire a new home, car, business or other personal investment.

Retail Advertising Schemes

Beware of retail sales advertisements. Buying a $50 item that is on sale for $40 is not a $10 savings if you did not need the item in the first place. It is actually an unnecessary $40 expense!

CALLING SCHEMES

A number of publications and 900 phone services list government surplus and different types of auctions at a cost of $30 to $100. Charging anything more than a few dollars for this information is an overcharge. And 900 calls are charged to you. Despite what you may think from these companies' ads, information on public and private auctions is free and readily available.

CLASSIFIED AD SCHEMES

Classified newspaper ads like the one below are often the opening pitch for what dozens of local Better Business Bureaus report as the fastest-growing category of consumer fraud:

LOAN SHARK SCHEMES

"Financial Problems? Bad Credit? No Credit? Loans/debt consolidations to $20K. 800-XXX-XXXX."

According to USA Today, New York City and Dallas each recently reported 4,000 complaints and inquiries; Phoenix had 6,000 and Cincinnati had 8,000. Consumers who respond are easily pre-approved for a loan. They'll receive it once they send an application fee or processing fee of several hundred dollars. The new loan, of course, never materializes.

State consumer protection agencies are finding that loan brokers are often a slippery bunch. Following thousands of complaints, Florida swiftly shut down more than 100 companies. But they soon show up in other states under different names.

ALWAYS ASK QUESTIONS

Ask questions, check the answers and consider all the facts before making that purchase or investing those hard-earned dollars. Always standing close by are those with their hands out, more than willing to take your savings from you. Don't let it happen to you. Be prepared, investigate and then invest!

So control your cash and watch it carefully so that it does not slip away from you! Do not co-sign for a loan or note, do what it takes to keep identity thieves away and don't get greedy winding up in a "get rich scheme."

Don't block your path to financial freedom! Control your cash!

Key Three

LIVE BELOW YOUR MEANS

*a*n oft-quoted axiom is "live within your means." That is good beginning advice for those who dive into heavy debt from living beyond their means, but such advice will hardly provide financially over the long haul.

To live a life that is debt free, bondage free and to head happily toward a comfortable retirement requires a different pattern of living. Financially, you must live below your means.

If you have been living above your means, you are already in serious debt and have no hope of becoming debt free unless you quickly change your financial habits. If you have been living within your means, you may be debt free, but you have little or no savings or investments to carry you through your retirement. What you must begin to do is live below your means.

Why is this important? Unless you believe you will be in excellent health to work in your 90s to provide food for yourself, shelter and the other necessities of life, you need to save and invest for your retirement years. Doing this is not possible if you are living above your means or simply living within your means.

If a person or family will live a restrained lifestyle, they will be able to live on thousands of dollars less each year. You should only incur debt when it makes good economic sense. The expense of borrowing should be less than the economic benefit that you will receive.

If you spend more than you earn, you have a very serious problem on your hands – the problem is you! Most people do not have an income problem; they have a spending problem. It' s not what you make; it's what you spend.

If you have managed to tame the spending tiger within you and are living within your means, you still have further cutbacks to make in your family cash flow. You need to spend below your available income stream. You need to be planning for your retirement.

Your government social programs won't provide adequate income for your retirement days – that will be left up to you. It is your responsibility, not your friends, family or government.

If you are like many people, you'll find that from time to time cash flow seems to come to a screeching halt just before payday. Actually in several cases, it seems to dwindle just after the paycheck arrives. Are you anything like that? Do you regularly find yourself in a cash crunch just before payday?

Do you find yourself juggling money between savings and checking because you can't maintain an adequate checking account balance? Perhaps you let one bill payment each month slide into next month. Or, even if your bills seem to be under control, you find it impossible to save any money. Does it sometimes feel like you have "holes in your pocket" that always allow the money to slip through? If so, welcome to life!

Some financial advisors recommend a rigid approach to spending: a certain percentage of income for housing, so much for food, this much for installment debt and so on. But others take a simpler and more flexible approach, dividing expenses into needs and wants. These figures taken from USA Today show national averages in various spending categories.

22%	Housing (including furniture and repairs)
22%	Transportation (car, gas and oil, repairs)
15%	Food
09%	Social Security, pensions
07%	Utilities
05%	Clothing
05%	Entertainment, recreation
04%	Medical care
03%	Savings
02%	Insurance (except car and home)
06%	Miscellaneous

Your first priority is to tithe the tenth (10 percent) that belongs to God. Tithe to your local house of worship. This is the place you receive your spiritual care. Next put away 10 percent for savings and investing.

Take care of yourself by setting goals, then treating those payments as fixed expenses. Suppose you have two children to put through college and you want a comfortable retirement. The first checks you write each month should be to your IRA, 401(k) and college savings plans.

Then come your living expenses. Roughly 70 percent of your money is already spoken for by needs such as rent or mortgage, utilities and taxes. Those are pretty much fixed expenses, although you can reduce taxes with proper planning.

Once needs are met, there's about 10 percent left over for debt reduction and other wants and that's where you begin making choices. You can buy new cars or used ones. Food is very discretionary—you can choose to eat very well or just a basic menu.

And clothes—you need appropriate clothing for work, but after that there is a lot of leeway. Every type of expense requires similar thinking. For instance, some heavy readers stock up on books and subscriptions, but you can use the library instead and save money.

SPENDING LESS

Okay, now you understand the necessity of living below your means. What does that really mean? In a nutshell, it simply means you have to spend less money than you earn. It means you do not allow yourself to spend money on things you don't absolutely need or things that just make you happy for a moment or two. It means you save money instead of spend it. It means investing the money that is left over.

The picture of retiring early, gaining wealth and having plenty of money to give to worthy causes is a picture of a happy life. You are the lender, not the debtor. You are the master, not the servant, because you have learned to master yourself. You have learned to discipline your sudden impulses and you have learned the difference between wants and needs. It's not complicated; it's very straightforward. It's living a simpler lifestyle.

A couple of years ago, my wife asked me if I had heard of the financial talk-show host, Dave Ramsey. I had not. On her way home from work each day, she regularly tunes into the show. On the way home, my sixteen-year-old son also listens to and likes the show. My son, Nathaniel, has always been a money-conscious young man who has been aware of price comparisons, spending habits and financial matters.

Since about the age of two, he has always been interested in and commented about things having to do with money. At the early age of about four, he chastised me for purchasing a box of ice cream bars when I could have purchased another box, with more bars in it for less money.

Of course, at that age, he didn't understand the difference between bars containing ice milk or real ice cream. To this day, he continues to ask questions almost daily about what we spend, how much we owe, will we be able to retire, etc. He seems to have been born with some kind of financial interest gene. At any rate, I now tune my radio to the Dave Ramsey Show on Sundays during our drive home from church. Nathaniel delights in anticipating the answers to the call-in questions before the host responds to the caller.

I like what Dave Ramsey says about living simply. He often notes, "If you will live like no one else, later you can LIVE like no one else." It's a great maxim and one that is true!

The authors of *The Millionaire Next Door*, Thomas Stanley and William Danko, have spent considerable time in researching the lives of the affluent and the wealthy. Their research led them to the following conclusions about how the rich in America arrived there, and how they continued to stay that way. From their conclusions, they believe the first point is the most important.

- They live below their means.
- They allocate their money, free time and energy to wealth accumulation.

- They prefer achieving financial independence over displaying / flaunting their social status.
- Their parents did not give them free and frequent handouts of money.
- Their children usually become self-sufficient.
- They are skilled in targeting business opportunities.
- They carefully select occupations that complement their skills and talents and that lead to building wealth.
-

Their studies show that typical millionaires own their own homes but do not live in multi-million dollar homes or drive expensive cars. More often than not, they buy used cars, bargain for other purchases and live simple lives. They do not live extravagant lifestyles. They usually live frugally.

Seldom do inheritances or advanced degrees build fortunes. The wealthy in America are usually living far below one's means and working very hard. Typical millionaires are willing to give up status to instead invest for financial security. The greatest percentage of millionaires are self-made.

They are some of the most efficient and resourceful people around. In many cases their children are unaware of their family's wealth. Instead of living in plush New York garden apartments, Beverly Hills or on the Florida waterfront, much of the time, they just live next door in comfortable neighborhoods.

Many millionaires are ordinary people who work dull jobs. They have learned important truths: nothing is more valuable than working hard, save large sums of money and live well below your means. They have learned the important lesson of living on a budget, accounting for their expenditures and paying close attention to their investments.

The only way for you to provide for your later years is to live below your means. If you want to have any hope of achieving financial independence you must live far, far below your means. This is not a difficult concept to understand. Although it is very simple, few people do it. Because it is so simple, people tend to discount its effectiveness.

The bottom line is this. There is no free lunch, no schemes by which you can get rich quick, no ship coming your way, no lottery with your name on it, and no alternative to plain, old-fashioned hard work.

In our culture, impulse buying is predominant. In years predating the present easy credit, you would walk into a department store, see an item you would like to purchase, and put a small cash down payment toward it and then pay it off monthly until the item was paid for. Once paid for, you took it home and began to enjoy it.

Many today fear that without the newest cars, latest toys and exotic vacations, they are missing the train. They find out later that by buying these things, they risk being run over by the train; the fast charging, mounting-debt train that's about to steamroll over their lives.

In our culture, credit purchases are the norm. Often, before an item has been paid for, it has been discarded. If you think you must have it all now or you cannot be happy, a paradigm shift must be made in your thinking. In our culture, going in hock up to our eyeballs is the normal thing to do. Our culture and society is all about promoting credit, spending, debt and a "I can have it now" way of life.

Buy now, think it through later. Buy now, worry about payment later. Live for today, let tomorrow's worries come later. Beginning a debt-reduction program almost seems counterculture.

You can build a huge nest egg for your later years simply by living below your means. Does it mean driving a car that should be abandoned in a junkyard? Not really. Does it mean eating oatmeal seven days a week and drinking only water? Not really, but perhaps that would help you with your weight-loss goals.

It does mean monitoring your spending, watching your cash and accounting for every penny spent. It means making conscious financial decisions based upon need and stopping your impulse spending. It means waiting 30 / 60 days before purchasing, giving you time to come to your senses.

TOO MUCH DEBT

Americans are literally trillions of dollars in debt. That is the danger of credit, which is simply the ability to borrow money. In short, it is the spending of money today that will be tomorrow's income. Most economists would say that credit is an important part of the ability of individuals, families, cities and ultimately nations to function in a financial world. Credit consists of unpaid balances on auto loans, credit cards, student loans and generally any non-mortgage debt.

One of the real dangers of excessive borrowing is that it creates high monthly payments, which often strain even well-planned budgets. The pace of borrowing often exceeds the family's growth in income and leads to a form of credit-debt bondage. The interest expense of credit debt is often very high. Banks and other lending institutions often will loan to people with a higher credit risk, but do so at the expense of the borrower.

This is a huge profit opportunity for the company. Often those that do not qualify for the terms of a regular loan still get money, but at an interest rate several points higher than normal. Of course, most individuals, families and businesses will quickly agree to this because, in reality, they need the money at any cost.

People that have high monthly credit payments often sacrifice their other financial goals just to make their payments. This is a very serious offense. By not investing in a house, savings account or other forms of investment, they seriously put their future retirement in question.

Excessive debt cannot be ignored. It will not go away. You can ignore past-due bills, but you do so at the risk of finding yourself in even worse circumstances. A chain of events is triggered when you do not pay your bills. Creditors can take action against you, the past-due bills can be turned over to a debt collector, your property can be repossessed and your wages garnished.

While debt bondage is the result of unwise decisions and excess credit purchases, there is no easy way out. The reason why people find themselves in this position is because they spend more than they earn and the only way out is to spend less and pay the difference on their debt balance.

The only way out of this dangerous situation is to get control of your spending and put yourself on a budget, which we defined earlier as a written plan that provides oversight and guidance to your spending habits.

DON'T BE A CREDIT RISK

People who live above their means quickly become credit risks. Everyone knows that potential lenders look closely at your credit record, but did you also know that landlords and insurance companies do, too? Here are some tips for building up a clean credit record—and making sure it stays that way.

You probably already know that your credit report is all-important when it comes to qualifying for any type of loan, including a mortgage, an auto loan or a low-rate credit card, but you may not realize that having a lousy credit rating (or credit score) can impede you when it comes to getting a job, renting an apartment or even getting a decent rate on auto insurance.

Landlords, employers and insurance companies have all discovered that someone who pays their bills on time is likely to be responsible enough to pay their rent and insurance obligations as well; become good employees and responsible enough to drive safely on the roads. That means it's in your best interest to keep your credit report—and your credit score —in its best possible condition.

Now you probably know that your credit report is essentially your credit history. It details what sort of loans you have outstanding, how long you've had them, whether you pay your bills on time and so on. (The information is not just from credit card companies, but all your creditors including utilities, landlords, hospitals, banks, etc.)

Your credit score, however, is more complicated. It's a computer-based determination of the risk you pose to each of your creditors. In fact, it's calculated differently for each lender, using those particular parts of your credit report that are thought to be the most telling.

According to Fair, Isaac & Co., a leading supplier of credit data, these scores include up to 100 factors, including the number of times you've paid bills 60 days late, the size of your credit line (particularly the part that isn't being used), the number of recent inquiries into your credit history (an indication that you're looking for more credit) and any bankruptcies, liens and foreclosures.

Fortunately, the rules were recently changed and you can now take a look at both your credit report and see your credit score. You can also improve your score (and your overall credit history) with some fairly simple maneuvers, which will be covered later.

WISE CREDIT MANAGEMENT

In the process of building our financial future, there are times when we ask another person or a financial institution to use their money for a limited period of time. This is borrowing or taking out a loan. Usually, the lender allows us to use their money in exchange for a percentage fee called interest. Our generation seems to be caught up in easy credit because of the ready money available.

There are very few people (if any) who do not worry that money may be going out the door faster than it is coming in. Most Americans have revolving credit balances from credit cards and other retail establishments and a small group are enslaved to mountainous consumer-debt burdens that eat at large parts of their income. Whether you are moderately in hock or in a deep hole—you can break that debt cycle.

At one time (a few years ago), it may have made some sense to borrow. You could deduct interest payments from your income taxes. With the cost of living running at 8 to 12 percent a year, you could repay your loans with cheaper dollars later. But now tax deductions for interest on consumer purchases have dried up. Inflation seems to be under control, meaning that expensive dollars remain expensive; and you can't count on huge raises in personal income a couple of times a year.

In spite of some lower interest rates available, credit card companies continue to charge extremely high interest on the unpaid balances. At the same time, passbook saving accounts pay so little, it is hard to see an advantage to them.

Falling behind on repaying lenders will only serve to hurt your credit rating. Late payments can remain on your credit file for seven years. Even if you do pay on time, having too much installment debt compromises your ability to borrow for something important in the future. If the whole country is in a recessionary economy, the last thing you should have is a lot of debt.

In order to be free from all those creditors, admit the problem in this area and stop borrowing. You too, as others, may be a spendaholic. Do you have too many credit cards? Do you like to shop too much? Is it hard for you to resist a so-called bargain?

LIMITING YOUR USE OF CREDIT

How much debt is just too much? A call to a consumer credit counseling service yielded this advice. Spending more than 15 percent to 20 percent of net income on monthly debt payments, not including your payments on a home mortgage, is just too much.

Easy availability of credit is partly to blame for many problems. Creditors are not the tight-fisted people they were years ago. It is common to receive several offers for credit cards each week in the mail. All you need to do is sign the offer and return it for instant credit. Potential creditors insure consumer credit with unparalleled leniency. After all, it's hard for them not to make money with interest rates of 18 percent or more.

People who use credit cards as a receipt process and then pay their outstanding balance in full each month will avoid trouble. Credit card companies disguise potential debt problems. It is tough to spot trouble when the minimum monthly payment required reflects only 3-5 percent of the total balance. One can be dangerously in debt before any difficulties are noticed.

While it is illegal for creditors to send you unsolicited credit cards, they can increase the limits or lines of credit without asking. For people who have difficulty in controlling their spending habits, more credit means more debt, which means more trouble.

Living above your means creates high stress levels. High stress levels affect your health, your spiritual life, your emotional health, your marriage and your financial life. Living within your means lessens this stress. Living below your means decreases the normal stress of life much more. Living far below your means gives you peace of body, soul and spirit.

Don't block your path to financial freedom! Begin to live below your means!

Key Four

SAVE FOR YOUR FUTURE

*Y*ou may be reading this book at a very young age, but you'll get old very quickly, trust me. Someday all of us want to relax and not have to focus on earning money every hour of every day. The best way to prepare for that time in our lives is to begin saving at an early age. Saving while young is simpler, requires less, is habit-forming and much, much easier. This is not rocket science, it's just simply having time on your side.

What kinds of thoughts come to your mind when I mention the word "saving" to you? Are you immediately having thoughts of dislike, pain, going without, not having any fun, or living cheap? Does it seem you just aren't ready to cope with great sacrifice? Or does the word saving have a different feel? Maybe for you it means being prepared for emergencies or planning for retirement.

Maybe to you it feels like financial freedom and easy living in your later years. It might even give you dreams of wealth and prestige. Regardless of whatever thoughts come to your mind when you think of beginning a savings plan, the fact remains that there is a definite relationship between saving now and future wealth. You may give up a little of your spending power now, but doing so will yield a whole lot more later. Continually and consistently saving and investing money now will lead to big rewards later.

The secret to becoming wealthy is steady plodding; putting away a few dollars at a time, consistently, week after week for the rest of your life. Adjusting your lifestyle to do this is not only important, but also absolutely necessary. To start saving for the future, you also have to find some money to save. This, of course, mandates that you live below your means; i.e., spend less than you earn.

"How can I begin to save?" you ask. "Where will I get the money?" Basically, you can begin your savings or increase your savings in three ways. First, you can find savings money by reducing your regular expenses. Do without some things you normally buy. Perhaps it's that daily latte or the fast-food snacks.

Second, you can find savings money by increasing your income. This may mean a part-time job, or some weekend service you can provide. It might even be a raise or bonus from your regular job.

Third, you can find money to save by converting unused / unneeded possessions (assets) into cash. This may be as simple as selling something to a friend or family member (one man's trash is another man's treasure); it may mean having a garage sale, or it can mean getting rid of that adult recreational toy you rarely use. Either way, these three basic options can put savings money into any person's pocket.

Savings and investments are necessary for you to take full responsibility for your future. You provide for your future by accumulating enough wealth to take care of your needs independent of any other person or entity. You accumulate wealth by investing. You invest by first saving dollars for that purpose. You save dollars by finding money to set aside in a savings vehicle.

You find money to set aside by living below your means. You live below your means by spending less than you earn. It is very important to begin setting aside money NOW. It does not matter whether you are old or young, now is the time to begin. Tomorrow never seems to come. Of course, by starting at an early age, time is on your side.

The following chart shows the annual return on an investment in five-year increments. Of course, one could start at age 50 and have $132,683 by the time he reaches the age of 75. Later, I will chart for you the benefits of starting very young and what the effects of a life of investing will do for you. If you were to begin saving now, an amount of $100 per month, the following chart details your possible investment return showing a variety of percentages and years.

Annual Return	5 Years	10 Years	15 Years	20 Years	25 Years
1.5% Bank Account	$6,226	$12,938	$20,171	$27,968	$36,372
5.0% Money Market Fund	$6,800	$15,528	$26,728	$41,103	$59,550
10.0% Stock Mutual Fund	$7,743	$20,484	$41,447	$75,936	$132,683

After looking forward to it for many years and planning for it with anticipation, your years of retirement should be a time of enjoyment and a wonderful season in your life. But when the time comes, will you have all of the resources accumulated to allow you to live the life you imagined?

Most people will have to replace 70-80% of their current income at retirement age. Many will want to replace 100% of their pre-retirement income. Because we are living longer and healthier lives, we can expect to live 20 plus years after retirement and to be more active at an older age than previous generations.

Then there is the inflation factor. Your accumulated nest egg will be worth much less in purchasing power because of it. Suppose we have an average annual rate of inflation of 4%. If you have $20,000 in current savings, that $20,000 would have to grow to $43,800 to have the same purchasing power 20 years from now.

There are a number of ways that derail the best of intentions. Many find themselves on track with their savings and investments and well on their way to financial independence, then something happens. It might be something as simple as your "wants" getting in front of your "needs."

One of your "needs" is to provide for your future. It may be a major health problem that sucks up your savings and investments. It is important to do preventive maintenance in this area. Be sure to have adequate health insurance at all times. Don't ever be without it. You also need disability insurance coverage.

Other possibilities that might drain your savings are short-term emergencies. Financial emergencies happen in life. You will never be able to predict just when it will happen, how it will happen or where it will happen. But it is a fact of life that it will happen. Without an emergency fund set aside, you are unprepared, and it can be costly and worrisome.

These needs might be new tires for your vehicle, a shortfall in seasonal income, an unexpected house repair – the list could go on forever. Many people face these inconvenient expenses by raiding their savings or retirement funds.

Though cash flow challenges are sure to surface, the answer is not to dip into savings or investments. The answer is to have a separate savings account that is pre-designated for such emergencies. Even before saving for your retirement or preparing for investments, it is of utmost importance to set aside an emergency fund.

Though ultimately you will want to have three to six months income set aside in this fund, beginning with at least $500-$1000 will get you started. Depending on your education, experience, job skills, time on the job, etc., you will eventually need up to six months of income saved. Of course, if you are paid on commission or are self-employed, six months might be a minimum to set aside in an emergency fund.

Investing while you are still young has many pluses. If, for instance, you invest at age 22, even if your total contribution is limited, observe what you can still end up with after just putting aside $2,000 per year for only six years. In this example I am using an average return of 12%.

Contribution Amount	Total Accumulation	Age / Number of Years
$2,000	$2,240	22/1
$2,000	$4,509	23/2
$2,000	$7,050	24/3
$2,000	$9,896	25/4
$2,000	$13,083	26/5
$2,000	$16,653	27/6
$0	$18,652	28/7
$0	$20,890	29/8
$0	$23,397	30/9
$0	$41,233	35/14
$0	$72,667	40/19
$0	$128,064	45/24
$0	$225,692	50/29
$0	$397,746	55/34
$0	$700,965	60/39
$0	$1,235,339	65/44
$12,0000	Total Cash Contribution	Contributing 6 Years

Now let's assume you don't begin to invest early. Note the following chart to see what would happen if you spent all your money from age 22 to age 27 and then decided that you should be investing $2,000 per year.

Contribution Amount	Total Accumulation	Age / Number of Years
$0	$0	22/1
$0	$0	23/2
$0	$0	24/3
$0	$0	25/4
$0	$0	26/5
$0	$0	27/6
$2,000	$2,240	28/7
$2,000	$4,509	29/8
$2,000	$7,050	30/9
$2,000	$25,130	35/14
$2,000	$56,993	40/19
$2,000	$113,147	45/24
$2,000	$212,598	50/29
$2,000	$386,516	55/34
$2,000	$693,879	60/39
$2,000	$1,235,557	65/44
$74,000	Total Cash Contribution	Contributing 37 Years

When you begin saving / investing at an early age, you have a lot of time on your side. Compound interest and / or investment growth can put a lot of money into your retirement pocket.

I have a 15-year-old son. Let's say that I made a one-time investment into a S&P 500 mutual fund of $1,000 when he was 12 years of age. (An S&P 500 index fund is a group of stocks considered to be generally representative of the stock market.

This index is composed of 400 industrial, 20 transportation, 40 utility and 40 financial companies.) Assuming that neither he nor I ever placed another dime into his account, by the age of 65, at an annual growth rate of 12%, he would have an investment portfolio worth $406,027. Actually, this is exactly what we did.

Let's look at another scenario. What if I started with that initial investment of $1,000 in a mutual fund that averages a 12% return, compounded monthly. Now say that I set aside $150 each month to add to the fund. My son, should he continue adding to it in the same amount after I am gone, at the young age of 65, assuming he has no other investments whatsoever, his net worth would be $8,949,244.81. This also is what he and I are doing together. He contributes from his earnings and I pitch in with the rest. At age 75, he would have $29,570,476.09.

The secret of financial success is to spend what you have left after saving, instead of saving what is left after spending.

Long-term investing is your best hedge against inflation, but you need to save in order to invest. This can be tough to do. Have you ever noticed that after you pay your monthly bills, buy groceries and cover your other expenses, you have little left in your paycheck? Consider contributing to your savings plan first—not last—each month.

A THREE-PART STRATEGY

Saving money is hard work. And the hardest part is simply getting started. If you're beginning from scratch, consider this three-part strategy:

1. Save for the unexpected—three to six month's worth of living expenses. In case you lose a job or find yourself with no steady income, this rainy-day fund will become necessary. Take no chances with this money. Keep it readily available, in a bank account or a money-market mutual fund.

2. Save for long-range expenses—a new home or college for the kids. Be more flexible with this money. Keep it in long-term certificates of deposit or in Series EE Savings Bonds. You'll earn more interest than in a conventional bank account and you can time your investment so the money is available when you need it.

3. Save for retirement. That can mean an Individual Retirement Account, a company retirement plan, or other solid financial investments. A conservative mutual fund that invests only in top-quality stocks is one possibility. Or you might risk a little more for a greater reward by investing in a mutual fund that buys growth stocks.

AUTOMATED SAVINGS

The following steps can help you make this practice automatic:

Set up an automatic payroll deduction. Thanks to payroll deduction programs, such as credit unions or 401(k) plans, part of your paycheck can go directly into your investment account.

Set up an automatic bank transfer. Many investment companies will transfer money automatically from your bank account to your investment account according to a schedule that you specify. Such a program can make saving for retirement as natural as paying the mortgage.

Invest all salary increases. Direct half of your next raise into an investment account before it reaches your wallet and you get used to spending the extra income.

Invest lump sum payments. Invest a portion of bonuses and tax refunds; you'll turn the extra money into added savings—not increased spending.

A Few Starter Tips

Set Savings Goals

Start with 5-10 percent of every paycheck. It's easiest if your employer deducts it from your pay because you don't miss money you don't see. You could also ask your bank to move it from checking to savings every month or make automatic investments into a no-load (no sales charge) mutual fund.

Saving is more certain when someone else arranges it for you. The goal may be college for the kids. It may be retirement in a few years. It could be a new car, a boat or a summer place. A real key here is that it forces you to think ahead, beyond the next paycheck. Any successful business is one that plans for the future; many times, 5 and 10 years ahead. Japanese companies project plans even longer.

Pay Yourself First

After taking care of your tithing obligations, the next person in line to be paid is you. Although this seems very hard to do with all of our other obligations, just get started by forming a regular habit. It will get easier as you progress. Use direct deposit for automatic savings. It can be much easier to save when the money goes directly into a savings account.

In that way, the decision to save is out of your hands. What you don't see, you are not likely to miss as much.

AVOID SPENDING ON IMPULSE

Most of us save too little because we spend too much on impulse items. Control that urge to splurge. Keep a list of all the things you really need - coats for the kids, a new refrigerator, tires for the car, etc. But wait to buy until those items go on sale. If you're drawn to something not on the list, give yourself a week to think it over.

Saving is easy: What you don't see, you won't spend.

SAVE ALL EXTRA MONEY

Once you have paid off a loan, start paying yourself by putting an equivalent amount of money directly into savings. If you have a car loan you're about to pay off and you've been paying $250 a month, keep the car for a couple more years and save that $250 each month. Some people plan so there's a tax refund each year, but most financial planners suggest handling your taxes so you don't overpay. After all, Uncle Sam doesn't pay any interest on the overpayment.

Thrift used to be a basic part of the American ethic. Before we were a nation, Ben Franklin said, "A penny saved is two pence clear." All of us would benefit by returning to that thinking.

WAYS TO MAKE YOUR SAVINGS GROW FASTER!

Put cash you don't need right away in three- or five-year CD's. If you need the money and have to break into the CD before it matures, you might pay a six month interest penalty. But that's nothing compared with the penalty you're imposing on yourself by settling for today's low short term rates "just in case."

MONEY MARKET FUND

Keep the cash you use for big bills in a money market mutual fund instead of a bank account. You may get free checks and your money continues to earn interest until the check clears. As a rule, money funds pay from 0.5 to 2 percent more than the highest rate you can get with most banks.

STOCK MUTUAL FUND

Buy a mutual fund that invests entirely in U.S. Treasury securities. These are even safer than money market mutual funds and, if you live in a high tax state, they're a better deal. Although Treasury funds often yield a little less than other money market funds, you owe no state or local income taxes on your earnings, so your return is much higher.

U.S. TREASURIES

Buy Treasury securities instead of CD's if you live in a high tax state. You can buy Treasuries free through the nearest Federal Reserve bank or branch. Check your telephone book under U.S. Government or ask your own bank for the address. The minimum investment in Treasuries maturing in one year or less is $10,000; in two or three years, $5,000; in four years or more, $1,000.

Check your tax bracket carefully before buying tax-exempt mutual funds. You'll generally net more after taxes, by investing in higher yielding taxable funds if you're in the 15 percent federal tax bracket. Sometimes taxables pay for people in the 28 percent bracket too, but in the highest brackets, tax exempts are usually best.

17 Practical Ways to Save Your Money

▶ *1.Develop new habits.*

Become a skillful shopper. Regional retail centers are exciting places. In supermarkets, thousands of goods line the shelves and invite attention. It takes skill and determination to pass down the aisles and resist temptation. The skillful shopper prepares a shopping list before going to market and buys only those items needed.

Learn to read labels and interpret them. Make substitutions for the higher priced items, judge the value of the week's bargain offerings and decide whether the best buys are best for the family. Careful shopping can save many dollars a week in the budget.

▶ *2.Get rid of credit card debt.*

Here is a good way to save some big money fast. There is one great investment that is sure to pay off, yet we fail to recognize it, even though it's right in front of us every month. Pay off your credit cards! Let's say for example that you owe $2000 on a Visa card. Many charge cards still have an interest rate in the neighborhood of 19 percent.

Instead of taking that $2000 bonus check and investing it into some low-interest-paying bank account, pay off that credit card and get a great return on your money! By paying off the outstanding balance, it is the same as getting a check for $570 tax-free! And one more thing: be a real friend to yourself by cutting up the card and canceling your credit. You'll be glad you did! It's the best financial investment you can make.

If you're in the 30 percent state and federal tax bracket, paying off an 18 percent credit-card debt provides the same return as an investment that yields 26 percent! If you're in the 17 percent bracket, paying off credit cards is the same as earning 22 percent. Why keep money in a 5 percent (or less) savings account when it can earn 22 percent paying off your credit cards?

▶ *3. Use installment credit sparingly.*

Recognize that any installment purchase or loan means one more fixed expense in the budget. Although credit is readily available and most anything can be obtained, be wary of the low-down, low-monthly-payment offers. There may be times when installment purchases are unavoidable, but this kind of spending, if excessive, can become a costly way of providing for family needs or for achieving family goals.

▶ *4. Take good care of your assets.*

Clothes last longer and remain better looking if they are kept clean and pressed. Food lasts longer when it is properly stored. Equipment lasts longer and gives better service when used according to the manufacturer's instructions. It makes sense to prolong the use of one's possessions by taking care of them. The longer we can use an article, the more we are getting for our money.

▶ *5. Update your homeowner's policy.*

As a rule, you need to be covered for at least 80 percent of the cost of rebuilding your house. Otherwise you won't get full reimbursement even if a fire destroys only one room. Ask your insurance agent how to estimate the cost. If you rent, get tenant's insurance to cover furniture and other valuables. Many renters fail to do this, thinking losses will be covered by the landlord. Not so!

▶ *6. Update your life insurance policy.*

You need only enough to take care of your dependents if you die. If there is a non-bread winner in the family, generally stick with low-cost term insurance; then cut it back or cancel it when the children grow up. Primary breadwinners, by contrast, often have to provide for an aging spouse, so they may need some cash value insurance whose premiums won't rise as they get older. If you have no dependents, you don't need life insurance. Put cash into retirement funds or disability insurance instead. Disability insurance is overlooked by many people.

▶ *7. Start a retirement fund.*

If you work for a corporation which has one, use the 401(k) plan. If employed by a firm with no pension plan, open an Individual Retirement Account. As a rule, both the contributions to these plans and the earnings are untaxed until you withdraw the money, so tax savings help pay the cost. If you leave your job, you can take 401(k) savings with you. Do not fail to use these plans! They're the best route to independence in old age.

▶ *8. Get the best health insurance possible.*

If you aren't covered at work, try to participate in a group plan through an organization you belong to or can join. Alternatively, call Blue Cross/Blue Shield or a Health Maintenance Organization (check the yellow pages). If you can't afford what they offer, talk to an insurance agent about a high deductible policy that covers only major medical costs. (You pay the small bills, but the huge ones are covered.) Today's buyers often take deductibles of $1,000 to $5,000, which greatly lowers costs. Whatever you do, never buy insurance advertised by celebrities on TV; it's not worth the cost.

▶ *9. Pay off your home mortgage faster.*

All over America, homeowners are taking 15 year mortgages or making extra payments on long-term mortgages, which has the effect of shortening the term. Any homeowner who has taken a look at an amortization schedule realizes that a large part of their monthly payment merely covers the interest charges on the outstanding debt, instead of paying down on the original loan.

Faster payments do lower interest costs and allow you to own your home free and clear sooner. A paid-up home is the cheapest way to live in retirement. By making slightly larger monthly payments than your loan requires, you'll significantly reduce your total interest cost and pay off your mortgage years early. For example, send in $50 extra in advance every month on a $150,000, 30-year, ten-percent mortgage and you'll save $68,325 and reduce the term of your loan by more than five years.

While it is true that mortgage interest can offset your taxable income, this has limited value. The offset does not reduce the tax itself, rather it reduces taxable income. If you are in the twenty-eight percent tax bracket, a $100 mortgage-interest deduction will save $28 in federal taxes, $31 for you if you are in the thirty-one percent tax bracket and so on. The remaining part of that $100 mortgage ($72 or $69) interest payment is lost. Additionally, people with adjusted incomes well over $125,000 may not be allowed to deduct all of their mortgage interest.

Instead of making only the minimum payment required by a lender, many people today are repaying their loans more quickly. One way to do this is to use a fifteen-year rather than a thirty-year amortization schedule. Another way is to prepay the mortgage either by making extra payments or by increasing the size of the regularly scheduled payments and specifying that the surplus should be applied to principal.

According to Spirit Magazine, adding a mere $10 a month to each payment, beginning in the third year of a $100,000 thirty-year mortgage at eight percent, can save $8,515 in interest charges and will pay off the debt sixteen months early.

David Ginsbury, president of Loantech, says, "Making just one pre-payment of principal a year can make a tremendous difference over time." He goes on to note that starting with the same $100,000 loan at eight percent for thirty years, a prepayment of $500 each December will cause the mortgage to be paid off twenty-nine months early, while one-time annual prepayments of $1,000 and $2,000 will retire debt in twenty-two years, seven months and eighteen years, eight months, respectively.

These results are so dramatic that it might seem as if every homeowner should begin prepaying immediately. But don't forget to first have about six months of income set aside as an emergency fund.

▶ *10. Use non-money resources.*

It is very easy to rely entirely on financial resources for all the goods one wants and needs. But this kind of thinking and living places a very heavy burden on the family income and often postpones the day when a goal can be achieved. However, by developing skills among family members and by substituting one's time, energy and skill in place of money, many services can be provided at home without dipping into the family funds. This kind of planning and achieving often provides far greater satisfaction than does the routine of shopping and buying.

▶ *11. If you want it to last, choose quality over price.*

Do you look for quality rather than just cost or appearance when you buy something that you want to last a long time? Do you save sales slips, guarantees and other records of purchases so you know where to find them? Do you buy at reliable stores that stand behind their merchandise? Read the labels on boxes, packages or other purchases to determine the real quantity or quality you are getting for your money. Instead of purchasing your wants immediately, put money aside to save for something you want but can't afford at the moment.

▶ *12. Pause before purchasing.*

Before spending your hard-earned resources, pause a while to ask yourself three simple questions.

A. Can I really afford it?

B. Do I really need it?

Whether or not you can afford it may be a simple matter of addition and subtraction—you either have enough money or you don't. But more often it will be a matter of deciding how important this particular purchase is compared to other purchases you may want to make.

There are many things we might like to have which would make life easier and more fun. Don't think you must always deny yourself all of these; after all, life is supposed to be fun as well as work. Many things that would have been considered luxuries in past years are now considered necessities. But you are going to have to pick and choose according to whatever your particular desires are. The more limited your budget, the more picking and choosing you are going to have to do. This is one of the harder facts of life.

C. Is it worth what I'm paying for it?

This is where spending money becomes a real skill. Worth or value is often hard to determine. Value in this case means the quality of the product itself; it also means the usefulness of the product for your particular purposes. You have to think about both. In determining value, price alone can be misleading. The lowest price may be the best value for your money, but then again it may not be. The highest price doesn't necessarily mean the best value either. Usually, you will find the best value somewhere in between.

Generally, when you are buying a product where length of service and performance are important, quality—how well it is made, how well it functions, how long it will last—is first consideration. Price is, within budget limits, a second consideration. Appearance may or may not be a consideration. If it's a suit or dress, yes; if it's an electric drill, probably not.

If you are buying a product where length of service is not so important—soap or paper plates, for instance—the lower price is usually the better value for your purposes. Quality is not as important, as long as what you buy does the job to your satisfaction. A lot of hard work and a little luck will stretch your dollars a little more. (The unit cost is most important here—how much does each paper plate cost?)

▶ *13. You can save by putting yourself to work:*

- Always switch off the lights when you leave a room.
- Borrow books from your local public library instead of buying them.
- Buy a used car rather than a new one.
- Buy holiday cards and decorations after Christmas at half price or less and save them for next year.

- Eat out at lunchtime rather than at dinner—it is usually at least 40 percent cheaper.

- Learn to give yourself haircuts and experiment cutting your family's hair.

- Practice the art of trading down: one step down in suits, in travel arrangements, in size of rental cars, etc.

- Return empty bottles to the supermarket and get back your deposit.

- Review insurance policies to avoid overlapping coverage.

- Save the plastic or paper bags from the supermarket to use as garbage bags.

- Take advantage of all free or low-cost offers: snacks at the supermarket, free visits to try out a health club, two-for-one meals at a restaurant, etc.

- Take up walking or jogging in the park or the street and avoid the cost of joining a health club. Use free city parks and tennis courts, instead of paid recreational areas.

- Wash your car yourself instead of taking it to the car wash.

- Wear a sweater at home during cool months, so that you can keep the thermostat turned down.

- When eating out, take advantage of the special fixed-price early dinners.

- When you become tired of some article of clothing, instead of disposing of it, put it aside for a season or two, then take it out again and it will look new.

- With relatives or friends, arrange for children's hand-me-downs to be saved and passed on from child to child.

▶ *14. Understand inflation.*

The rise in the price of goods and services, better known as inflation, can steadily erode the purchasing power of your income. That's why it's important to invest a portion of your savings. Inflation has been relatively tame in recent years. Since 1960, inflation has averaged 4.5 percent per year. Since 1988, it has averaged 3.5 percent per year. Still, no one can predict the direction of inflation rates, which could decline even more or return to the double-digit rates of the late 1970's and early 1980's. Even if inflation holds steady at 3.5 percent per year for 20 years, consumer prices will nearly double, as illustrated in the following table.

Item Purchased Today	Cost in 20 Years (4.5% average annual inflation rate)	Cost in 20 Years (3.5% average annual inflation rate)
Coffee & Scone - $7	$16.88	$13.93
Steak for 1 - $20	$48.23	$39.80
A Weekend Away - $500	$1,205.86	$994.89

▶ *15. Understand the power of compounding.*

Inflation can steadily erode the value of your income. Long-term investing offers the best antidote to inflation through the power of compounding.

Year after year, any money that you invest may earn interest, dividends or capital gains. When you reinvest those earnings, they help generate additional earnings. Those additional earnings help generate more earnings and so on. This is called compounding.

For example, if an investment returns 8 percent per year and its earnings are reinvested annually:

- After one year, your total return will be 8 percent.
- After five years, your cumulative total return will be 47 percent.
- After ten years, your cumulative total return will be 116 percent.

Best of all, the sooner you begin investing, the greater the compounding effect.

▶ *16. Begin saving while you are young.*

Consider the example of Dick and Jane, both 65 years old. They worked for the same company for 35 years and both invested in their employer-sponsored retirement plan. Jane started contributing at age 30. She invested $1,000 each year for ten years until the age of 40 and earned 8 percent per year. Then she stopped contributing; her investment continued to earn an 8 percent annual return. When she reached age 65, her $10,000 had grown to $107,100.

Dick postponed making contributions until age 40 and then invested $1,000 each year for 25 years. He also earned 8 percent per year. At the end of the period, his $25,000 investment was worth $79,000.

As you can see, although Jane contributed to her company plan for 15 fewer years than Dick and invested $15,000 less, she accumulated $28,100 more than Dick—simply because she started investing ten years earlier.

▶ *17. Learn how to invest.*

Saving and investing are often used interchangeably, but they are somewhat different. Saving is storing money safely—such as in a bank or money market account—for short-term needs such as upcoming expenses or emergencies. Typically, you earn a low, fixed rate of return and can withdraw your money easily.

Investing is taking a risk with a portion of your savings—such as by buying stocks or bonds—in hopes of realizing higher long-term returns. Unlike bank savings, stocks and bonds over the long term have returned enough to outpace inflation, but they also decline in value from time to time.

Don't block your path to financial freedom! Start saving for your future!

Key Five

GIVE TO OTHERS

*G*iving to others brings indescribable pleasure. An inward joy comes to you when you have reached out and helped others. Whether it be in monetary gifts or simply rolling up your sleeves and helping out the old-fashioned way, the act of giving brings its own reward.

Many readers of this book would not think their lifestyle is one of wealth and excess. To you the words extravagant and excessive would not seem descriptive of your standard of living. But the reality is that most of you really do live a life of abundance; you travel to where you wish, you buy what you desire and there are very few constraints in your lifetime of opportunities.

Dr. Neil Chadwick explains to us how really wealthy some of us are in the country of my origin (USA) in this excerpt from one of his messages.

"Recently it has come to my attention just how imbalanced a world we live in. The fact of the matter is, if you have food in the refrigerator, clothes on your back, a roof overhead and a place to sleep, you are richer than 75% of this world. If you have money in the bank, in your wallet, and spare change in a dish someplace - you are among the top 8% of the world's wealthy. If we could shrink the earth's population to a village of precisely 100 people, with all the existing human ratios remaining the same, 6 people would possess 59% of the entire world's wealth and all 6 would be from the United States; 80 would live in substandard housing; 70 would be unable to read; 50 would suffer from malnutrition; and only 1 would have a college education."

The Excitement of Giving

Giving is fun! Giving is exciting! Just try to give something away without feeling wonderful. The non-giver is a very miserable individual. When you are feeling blue and discouraged, try giving of yourself to others.

Give away something and discover what you receive in return. You will receive happiness, hope, a sense of peace and well being, and instant encouragement will come your way. Give even to your enemies. Drive them absolutely crazy with your selflessness and love.

Be a Good Steward

Stewardship is a biblical requirement for all Christians. It is all about blessing others, giving to others and practicing the art of putting good intentions to action.

Matthew 25:21

> *"His master replied, 'Well done, good and faithful servant! You have been faithful with a few things; I will put you in charge of many things. Come and share your master's happiness!'"*

The Bible is clear that our position in regard to property is as stewards, not owners. A steward is a guardian of the interests of another. The steward owns nothing, but carefully guards, protects and increases the property of the One he serves. The essential quality of a steward is faithfulness. When we are faithful, God gives us more because we have proven we are diligent to use what He gives us wisely and generously.

1 Chronicles 29:11-14

> *"'Yours, O LORD, is the greatness and the power and the glory and the majesty and the splendor, for everything in*

heaven and earth is yours. Yours, O LORD, is the kingdom; you are exalted as head over all. Wealth and honor come from you; you are the ruler of all things. In your hands are strength and power to exalt and give strength to all. Now, our God, we give you thanks, and praise your glorious name. But who am I, and who are my people, that we should be able to give as generously as this? Everything comes from you, and we have given you only what comes from your hand.'"

This prayer of David reflects the heart of a humble steward. He acknowledges that everything in heaven and earth belongs to God. He recognizes God as the head and ruler of everything, the giver of wealth and honor. God gives us things we may use, but ultimately everything belongs to God. The steward understands total dependence on God and gives generously to the Lord, simply from understanding that everything comes from Him.

GIVE YOUR TIME

Your personal time is very valuable. We know that. In our busy world of work, children, family, school, church and the like, our time might be the hardest thing to give. Yet, it is probably the most precious commodity we have. After all, our time on earth is short lived and we have only so much allotted to us. What we don't use wisely is gone forever.

When you give your time to others, they value it strongly. One of God's greatest gifts is time. Time is our tool. It is a wonderful gift. You can give this gift to others. Here are some examples of how you can give your time to others.

- Clean up litter in a neighborhood park.
- Take your family to a church maintenance day.
- Serve your church as greeters, ushers, teachers, filing clerks, etc.
- Gather and collect household items for the poor and needy.

- Clean an area of the church, either inside or outside.
- Bake a pie and deliver to your local firemen.
- Mow the grass of an elderly person.
- Visit the sick and incarcerated.
- Volunteer at a soup kitchen.
- Change the oil in the vehicle of a person who has been ill.
- Bake cookies or bread and take them to a shut-in or elderly person.
- Fix broken toys for children.
- Provide childcare for a single mother.
- Gather coats in the fall and distribute to needy families.
- Befriend a lonely person.
- Rake a neighbor's leaves in the fall.
- Prune rose bushes, plant flowers and help older people.
- Write a thank you note and send to your neighborhood police or fire station.

The list of what you can do with your time in service to others is endless. When you give to others you make a difference in their lives. Often you give them hope and encouragement they cannot find anywhere else. One should always have an attitude of service. This means being aware and anticipating the needs of someone else. This means offering to help instead of waiting to be asked. You serve God by helping others. God is giving to us continually. We can express His love to others by showing them genuine generosity.

GIVE YOUR MONEY

Exodus 35:5

"From what you have, take an offering for the LORD. Everyone who is willing is to bring to the LORD an offering of gold, silver and bronze..."

This verse advises us that a willing heart is a must for giving offerings. God gave us a freewill so we would love Him voluntarily. The same applies to our offerings. He doesn't demand we give more than the tithe, but when we give of our free will, we are telling Him we love Him and our desire is to worship Him with our offerings.

It is required you give to God the tenth of your increase that already belongs to Him, and it is always in our best interest to give above and beyond in offerings and designated gifts, so how else can we be involved in giving? I offer the following suggestions to consider in your giving perspective.

- Give to an overseas missions project.
- Give toward feeding the poor in your city.
- Give to help an unemployed family with their house payment.
- Give to a worthy charity.

Endless special projects and numerous charities could use your money and financial support. So how does one determine to whom to donate hard-earned money? We cannot help all the world, but we can help those with whom we are closest and those whom we have become aware of. Of course we can love the world, or help some overseas mission project, but can we love and help our neighbor? What kind of special needs do you have in your own neighborhood?

GIVE YOUR RESOURCES

A Mayan woman in Belize, Central America desired to give a gift to the missionary who had brought her the gospel. She knew the missionary's greatest need was money, though she had none to give for they did not use money in her village. She did not have livestock to give that could be eaten or even an extra portion of vegetables for the missionary to enjoy. All she had was the skill of her hands.

She made a living by weaving intricate tapestry and it took her 40 hours a week for an entire month to produce one. She decided she would work twice as much to produce an extra carpet to give. This offering blessed the missionary's heart more than any sum of money could have because it represented the woman's time, her skill and her heart.

Perhaps you do not have money to give. You can honor the Lord by offering your time and your skill. What are your skills? Are you good at typing? What about volunteering at the church office? Are you good at reading aloud to children? What about volunteering for story time in your church's children's ministry? Your church will probably be very blessed by the offering of your time and skill. There is always a way to give an offering – no matter how tight things are financially – so give with your heart.

Everyone has resources for giving. No, I am not talking about money, nor am I necessarily referring to time, though it could involve our time. I am speaking of those things that can be given for a specific purpose or at a specific time. What if you are a professional Nurse and you know of an elderly person who could use a medical visit from time to time.

You can give the gift of your vocation to those you know. Perhaps you are a carpenter and a single mom's porch is badly in need of repairs. Maybe you are a landscaper and you could lend a hand to a disabled household. Maybe you own a truck and a poor family needs a helping hand in moving to a new home. You may be a whiz at science or math and a young neighbor needs some extra tutoring. Get creative in giving your personal resources.

GIVE YOURSELF

We, as the Body of Christ are responsible for the health and welfare of all the parts of the Body. We are also responsible for reflecting the heart of Christ to those in need in our society. One of the most important ways we can give an offering to God, as revealed by the following passage, is by meeting a need. Check your local church to find out if you might be able to meet any needs.

Hebrews 13:16

"And do not forget to do good and to share with others, for with such sacrifices God is pleased."

GIVE BECAUSE YOU HAVE BEEN GIVEN TO

This thought is illustrated by the story of a small boy.

A little boy came into the kitchen one evening while his mom was fixing supper. And he handed her a piece of paper he'd been writing on. So, after wiping her hands on her apron, she read it, and this is what it said:

- For mowing the grass, $5
- For making my own bed this week, $1.
- For going to the store, $0.50.
- For playing with baby brother while you went shopping, $0.25.
- For taking out the trash, $1.
- For getting a good report card, $5.
- And for raking the yard, $2.

Well, she looked at him standing there expectantly, and a thousand memories flashed through her mind. So, she picked up the paper, and turning it over, this is what she wrote:

For the nine months I carried you, growing inside me, No Charge,

For the nights I sat up with you, doctored you, prayed for you, No Charge.

For the time and the tears, and the cost through the years, No Charge.

For the nights filled with dread, and the worries ahead, there's No Charge.

For advice and the knowledge, and the cost of your college, No Charge.

For the toys, food and clothes, and for wiping your nose, there's No Charge, Son.

When you add it all up, the full cost of my love is No Charge.

Well, when he finished reading, he had great big tears in his eyes. And he looked up at her and he said, "Mama, I sure do love you." Then he took the pen and in great big letters he wrote, PAID IN FULL.

GIVE BECAUSE GOD IS GOOD

Matthew 12:35

> *"The good man brings good things out of the good stored up in him, and the evil man brings evil things out of the evil stored up in him."*

When our hearts are filled with the goodness of God, we will give from that goodness. Let's allow our hearts to be filled with the following truths about God's goodness.

- God wants to bless your work. (Deuteronomy 28:12)
- God wants to make your work increase and prosper. (Deuteronomy 30:9)
- God will keep His promises to you. (Joshua 21:45)
- The Lord's mercy endures forever. (Ezra 3:11)
- The Lord wants to put His good hand upon you. (Nehemiah 2:8)

- God is good and upright. (Psalm 25:8, Psalm 34:8, Psalm 100:5)
- God does that which is good. (Psalm 119:68)
- God wants to show you His loving kindness. (Psalm 69:16)
- God is good to the pure in heart. (Psalm 73:1)
- God wants to give every good thing to you. (Psalm 84:11)
- God wants to give you good things and increase your business. (Psalm 85:12)
- God will be abundant in mercy toward you. (Psalm 86:5)
- God wants to give good gifts to you. (Matthew 7:11)
- God is gracious and compassionate. (Exodus 33:19, Exodus 34:6)
- God wants to bless you. (Psalm 21:3)
- God wants to allow His goodness to be with you always. (Psalm 23:6)
- God prepares good things for those who fear Him. (Psalm 31:19)
- God gives the power to get wealth. (Deuteronomy 8:18)
- God gives strength and power to His people. (Psalm 68:35)
- God gives life to the world. (John 6:33)
- God gives us richly all things to enjoy. (1 Timothy 6:17)
- God has the power to do anything. (Isaiah 40:21-22)
- God has the power to create something from nothing. (Psalm 33:6-9)
- God is sovereign and there is nothing too hard for Him. (Jeremiah 32:17-19)

Romans 8:31-33

> *He who did not spare his own Son, but gave him up for us all-how will he not also, along with him, graciously give us all things?*

Sometimes our immaturity as Christians shows when we stay in the "asking/demanding" mode and forget to offer thanks for all that Christ has given to us. Not only are we blessing daily with His benefits, but let us not forget the "ultimate" gift that He gave to us; His life.

GIVE AS OTHERS HAVE GIVEN

While the next few stories speak of individuals with great wealth, don't be so sure that when compared with historical data and the rest of today's world, that you shouldn't take notice. Regardless of whether or not you have great wealth, by the standards of most of the world's citizens, you are a wealthy person.

Myrna Rose Strand

Myrna Strand is a retired school teacher from Minneapolis who decided to give her estate to charitable causes. She says, "My estate will never be large enough to be able to build libraries, but it may be large enough to buy some books for a library." As a young girl, she was taught to give and willingly placed coins in the Sunday school offering envelope each week.

Throughout her life she has been generous with her money and her time, volunteering thousands of charitable hours to church and other charities. She continues, "I have always wanted the balance of my estate to go to charities. I believe in the idea that when you come into the world you come in with nothing, and you have an obligation to give back. You can't take it with you. I believe I should carefully manage the resources God has entrusted to me, to care for his world, his people, his creation and myself."

Paul White

BTD Manufacturing, Inc., a metal stamping and fabrication business was established by Paul White and Earl Rasmussen. Their goal was to have a company that would always honor its greatest assets; its people. Along with that was a commitment to charitable giving. The BTD Manufacturing Foundation was begun in the year 1988. The company's goal is to share the profits with people in need. A few years ago, Paul White also established his own donor-advised family fund named the White Family Foundation. The family's charitable interests are driven in large part by a belief that people of wealth are merely stewards of those dollars on behalf of God. He says, "God gave each of us specific gifts and talents. If we use these talents in earning dollars, then we need to share those dollars with others."

Sir John Marks Templeton

Sir John Marks Templeton is a Rhodes scholar and a Yale graduate. Early in the 40's he began to try his hand in the art of investment. He established his first mutual fund in 1954. Using this fund, he purchased international equities long before other American investors did so. This first fund of his proved to be very successful. A typical investment of $10,000 in the year 1954 would have grown to, without additional contributions, a whopping $3 million by the year 1992. It was in 1992 that he sold his company for more than $400 million.

Mr. Templeton today remains a faith-filled, religious, values-oriented Christian philanthropist. He has been known to pay professors if they would promote conservative values. He gives to universities to build character in the lives of young persons. He funds researchers who will connect faith and science.

He launched the Templeton Prize for Progress in Religion in the year 1972. The first award went to Mother Teresa, some six years before she won the Nobel Peace Prize. Other winners include just famous names as Billy Graham and Chuck Colson. In 2003 he launched the Templeton Honor Roll which distinguished 126 universities, departments, professors and textbooks that uphold conservative and traditional educational values.

Andrew Carnegie

Andrew Carnegie was one of the leading industrialist of America's 19th century. Building America's steel industry made him one of the greatest and riches entrepreneurs in history. But it was not always that way. He was born in Scotland, to the son of a weaver in 1835, in a city that was the center of the linen industry. After the industrial revolution took place, the steam-powered looms put thousands of craftsman out of work. This caused his entire family to go to work selling groceries and mending shoes. Fearing future economic survival, the family borrowed enough money to travel by ship to North America. They took up residence in Pittsburgh the iron-manufacturing center of the country.

Andrew's father found work in a cotton factory and Andrew became a bobbin boy at a pay rate of $1.20 per week. From that job he went on to become a messenger boy in the local telegraph office. Later he began working at the Pennsylvania Railroad as a private secretary and personal telegrapher for a salary of around $35 per month.

He once said, "I couldn't imagine what I could ever do with so much money." Excelling in his responsibilities, he soon became the superintendent of the Pittsburgh Division. During the Civil War he helped to supervise military transportation for the North. After the war he worked for the Keystone Bridge Company replacing wooden bridges with bridges built of iron. He began earning an annual income of $50,000.

Over the ensuing years he worked to convert iron to steel, using his own personal money and borrowing additional funds to build a new steel plant near Pittsburgh. His motto was, "watch costs and the profits take care of themselves". By 1900 his plant produced more steel than all plants in Great Britain. Financier J.P. Morgan sought to take over the Carnegie Steel Company and did so at a cost of $480 million, making Andrew Carnegie the richest man in the world.

In his book, The Gospel of Wealth, Andrew Carnegie talks about how change has come to this nation. He states, "The poor enjoy what the rich could not before afford. What were the luxuries have become the necessaries of life. The laborer has now more comforts than the farmer had a few generations ago. The farmer has more luxuries than the land-lord had, and is more richly clad and better housed. The landlord has books and pictures rarer and appointments more artistic than the king could then obtain". He wrote this in the year 1889. I wonder what he would write today.

After spending a lifetime accumulating wealth and fortune, his later years were spent in giving it away to institutions of science, education, charitable foundations, libraries, churches and culture. By the time of his death, he had donated approximately $350 million to various worthy causes. He often said, "The man who dies rich, dies disgraced". He used his money to help others help themselves.

Jiang Minde

Born in a mountain village in 1946, Jiang Minde searched for God and found the Christian faith. In 1984 he began to produce a food for child nutrition called "Future." His annual production has reached 8,000 tons of rice noodles. Although a wealthy man, he chooses to live a simple lifestyle, living in an ordinary house.

He states, "My money comes from God, it was given to me by God for safeguarding. Hence, I cannot spend it recklessly, but ought to help those in need. As long as I have enough to eat and for my own needs, it is sufficient." Yet when it come to meeting the many needs of those in poverty, Jaing Minde is very generous. Since 1985 he has given more than $1.69 million to charity. Jiang says this; "With my work, I want to genuinely represent the Christian spirit of love to our neighbor."

George Muller

Born in Prussia in 1805, the son of a revenue collector, George Muller spent childhood money foolishly, stole government money while his father was out and wandered into great sin. At ten years of age, his father sent him away to a cathedral school to be trained in the ways of a Lutheran clergyman. During this time he engaged in sinful practices; lying, cheating, gambling, gross immorality, and often spent his evenings in the taverns, then wandering the streets during early morning hours after becoming intoxicated with strong drink. This lifestyle led to imprisonment at the age of sixteen. After attending some Christian Bible studies in a friend's home, in time he sobered up, got married and begin to lead an exemplanary life. Muller began preaching in many towns and cities, winning many to Christ. He eventually became co-pastor at Gideon and Bethesda Chapels in Bristol, in 1832. The congregations grew and at the time of his death he had a congregation of about two thousand persons at Bethesda Chapel.

George Mueller also started a very large orphanage and became a man of great faith. His efforts to operate an institution that cared for the daily needs of destitute children, required great faith and trust in God as a daily provider. One night before going to bed his staff informed him that there was absolutely no food in the building for the children's breakfast in the morning. He told them to go ahead and set the table for the morning meal and then he went to pray.

Early the next morning, there came a knock on the door. A local baker was awakened during the night with an overpowering feeling that he must get up and bake bread for the children. A few minutes later another knock on the orphanage door. The local dairyman's delivery cart had broken down in the neighborhood. Knowing that the milk would spoil before the cart could be repaired, he asked Mueller if he would take the milk off his hands. Of course the children never went hungry…not even for a single day.

In addition to the orphanages, Muller started the Scripture Knowledge Institution for Home and Abroad. Its purpose was to aid Christian schools, assist missionaries, and to circulate the Scriptures. At the time of his death 282,000 Bibles and 1,500,000 Testaments had been distributed and 112,000,000 religious books, pamphlets and tracts had been circulated. At the age of seventy, George Muller began a trek of evangelistic tours. Traveling over 200,000 miles and around the world he spoke to thousands of people. He continued traveling until the age of ninety.

A man who built great orphanages in England, did so with a vision from God and 50 cents in his pocket. He never made his needs known to man, praying only to God. Over $7 million was sent to him for ministry including the building and the maintaining of these orphan homes. At the time of his death, these five immense homes for orphans housed more than two thousand orphans.

After spending his last 17 years speaking to the nations, he died at the age of 93, leaving an estate valued at less than one thousand dollars. Yet he had given the Institute almost one-half million dollars of personal honorariums he had received during his ministry.

Saint Nicholas

Nicholas, born in Patara which is now Turkey, was the son of wealthy parents who raised him to be a devout Christian. Taking the words of Jesus literally when he told the rich young ruler to "sell what you own and give the money to the poor," Nicholas did just that. He took his entire inheritance and assisted the needy, the sick and those who were suffering.

After dedicating his life to serving God, in time he was made the Bishop of Myra. He became known as one who gave generously to people in need. Also known as well for his love for children and his concern for sailors. He was persecuted for his faith by the Roman Emperor Diocletian and subsequently exiled and imprisoned. Upon release he attended the Council of Nicaea in 325 AD.

James Cash Penney

This man's name became associated with doing business according to the Golden Rule. Born in 1875 into a poor farm family, he was a boy with plenty of self-discipline, very self- reliant and much personal character. Having to purchase his own clothing at the age of eight and needing a pair of shoes, he saved $2.50 earned from running errands, selling junk and performing any farm tasks available to him. He began to invest his earnings by buying and selling pigs, raising watermelons, horse trading and very quickly learned the ways of an entrepreneur.

His post high school career included clerking at a local dry goods store and investing in a butcher shop. Because he would not provide the chef of the local hotel with a weekly bottle of bourbon, he lost his biggest account and the butcher business soon failed. After that he went to work for the Golden Rule Stores and soon became a business partner in one of their new stores in Wyoming.

Before opening the store he studied the town and their needs, stocked the shelves with quality merchandise. It was an instant success. In subsequent years, James Cash Penney purchased all of the stores and opened more. In all of his stores he insisted on offering the lowest possible prices on the very best merchandise. At the end of 1912 he had opened 34 stores with sales in excess of $2 million. In the 1920s there were 197 J.C. Penney stores with sales of nearly $43 million. At age ninety, J.C. Penney maintained a full schedule of appointments and at the age of 95 still traveled to his 45th floor office and worked three days each week.

In 1911, Mr. Penney donated $10,000 to the First Methodist Church in Salt Lake City. In 1923 he established a 120,000 acre experimental farming community in northern Florida. This was divided into small plots where industries and moral, but economically destitute farmers could live and work and rebuild their lives.

In 1925 he established the J.C. Penney Foundation which funded such ministries as adoption agencies, homeless shelters, youth clubs, vocational libraries, family guidance centers, missionary projects, peace organizations and health clinics. Next to this he established the Memorial Home Community which is a 60 acre residential community for retired ministers, lay church workers, missionaries, their wives and families. In later years he donated to many other organizations including the National 4-H clubs, Junior Achievement and other community needs.

John D. Rockefeller

Born in 1839 in New York, John Rockefeller had a mother who was very religious and very disciplined. She taught him to work hard, save much and become a generous giver to charities. At age 12 he had saved $50 working for neighbors and raising turkeys. At the age of 16 he became an assistant bookkeeper with a merchant and produce shipper. At the age of 20 he went into business with a neighbor to form a company that traded in grain, hay, meats and other goods. From there it was the oil refining business and then the creation of the Standard Oil Company of Ohio.

From the mid 1890s until his death in 1937, Mr. Rockefeller was consumed with philanthropic activity. His fortune had peaked in 1912 at nearly $900 million. He began to give away hundreds of millions of dollars. Largely responsible for creating the University of Chicago, he pitched in a mere $75 million in 1932. Also in the 1930s he set up the Rockefeller Institute for medical research and his gifts totaled $50 million. He gave more than $530 million to various educational, scientific and religious institutions. This included gifts to Baptist institutions, the Y.M.C.A., Anti-Saloon League and colleges.

When asked about his giving his response was, "Yes, I tithe, and I would like to tell you how it all came about. I had to begin work as a small boy to help support my mother. My first wages amounted to $1.50 per week. The first week after I went to work, I took the $1.50 home to my mother and she held the money in her lap and explained to me that she would be happy if I would give a tenth of it to the Lord. I did, and from that week until this day I have tithed every dollar God has entrusted to me. And I want to say, if I had not tithed the first dollar I made I would not have tithed the first million dollars I made. Tell your readers to train the children to tithe, and they will grow up to be faithful stewards of the Lord. "

John D. Rockefeller once said, "Every right implies a responsibility; Every opportunity, an obligation, Every possession, a duty."

Martha Berry

The Boys Industrial School was begun on land Martha Berry deeded for that purpose. As founder of the Lavender Mountain school in Georgia, she was an educator who began teaching poor children before public schools were common. Using her own personal money to fund teachers and the educational budget, the school grew quickly and the quality of student education became well known even to presidents.

In future years other schools were opened that accepted girls as well. The Berry Schools accomplished so much that she founded Berry College in 1926. Martha Berry shared her time, money and gave her life so that poor children could be educated. Her life was one of focus and attaining great goals. A devout Christian, she believed that prayer combined with personal sacrifice and generous giving could accomplish much.

Bill & Vonette Bright

Founders of Campus Crusade for Christ, a ministry dedicated to sharing the gospel with every person on the planet, Bill and Vonette Bright have lived a life of service to Christ. After giving his heart to God, in 1951 he received a vision to begin evangelism on college campuses worldwide. Campus Crusade has grown to over 26,000 full-time staff members and more than 500,000 volunteers. Campus Crusade is active in 191 countries. Today Campus Crusade is the largest evangelical organization in the USA. The JESUS film was originated, distributed and translated into 800 languages.

The prestigious Templeton Prize for Progress in Religion was awarded to them in 1996. Instead of using the prize reward for personal enjoyment, they used the $1.1 million dollars to promote the spiritual discipline of fasting by teaching others how to do so with success. With a 2001 annual ministry budget of $437 million, Bill and Vonette Bright's combined income in 2002 was $50,570. Even though Bill Bright has written more than 60 books, all royalties have been given by him to Campus Crusade. Additionally, he has never accepted any speaking fees or honorariums. During his lifetime he gave away millions of dollars of personal income so that the world could be reached for Christ.

William Colgate

William C. Colgate was born in 1783, the eldest of five brothers. He came to America at the age of 12 with his father. In 1849, at the age of 16, William left home carrying his meager possessions. Meeting an old canal-boat captain, he told the old man how his father was too poor to support him anymore and that the only trade he was familiar with was that of making of soap and candles.

Kneeling, the old man prayed for the boy and then told him that someone would become the leading soap-maker in New York and it might as well be him. He urged William to give his heart to Christ. He instructed the young man on how to make a good quality of soap and give a full honest pound. He said that if he did so, he would become a prosperous and rich man.

Going into the city William united with a church. He became employed in a business, and soon became a partner and later sole owner of the business. Tithing on the very first $1 dollar he made, he continued to give to the Lord. He instructed his bookkeeper to open a separate account with the Lord's money. As the business prospered and grew, he soon began to tithe 20%, 30%, 50% and finally gave all of his income to the Lord. Eventually he gave millions to the Lord's work around the world.

During his lifetime he organized several Bible societies including the American Bible Society in 1816 and gave generously to a New York institution of higher learning later called Colgate University.

Henry P. Crowell

Founder of the Quaker Oats Company, and one who packaged and branded oatmeal into a worldwide brand, Henry Crowell built the company into a 250 million dollar business. As a Chicago businessman, it is said that over a period of 40 years, he gave away 70 percent of his earnings to church and charity. During his lifetime he led many business acquaintances to Christ.

Katharine Drexel

Saint Katharine Drexel was born in 1858 the daughter of wealthy railroad businesspersons. Katherine was the second daughter of Francis Anthony and Hannah Langstroth Drexel. One month after her birth, her mother passed away. It is said that she was taught from a very early age to use her assets and benefit others in need.

Growing up, her family shared their home with the poor several days a week. In 1891, Katherine founded the Sisters of the Blessed Sacrament and later founded many other ministries. Over the years she used her wealth to found and staff many schools for both Black and Native Americans, including Xavier University. Her older sister Elizabeth founded a trade school for orphans in Pennsylvania.

A younger sister founded a liberal arts and vocational school for poor blacks in Virginia. Over her lifetime, Katharine gave systemic aid to Indian missions, spending millions of her family fortune to help them. Donating over $20 million of her own money she began black Catholic schools in 13 states, 40 mission centers, 23 rural schools, 50 Indian missions, and Xavier University in New Orleans, Louisiana.

Jack Eckerd

The founder in 1952 of one of the largest drug store chains in the world, Jack Eckerd was a devout Christian who took his fortune and invested it in numerous charities. He funded a private college later becoming known as Eckerd College. Eckerd Youth Alternatives, which he began as a network of wilderness camps for at-risk youth, now operates 39 residential and community programs in 7 states. More than 65,000 youth have been through the program. Nearly $65 million in funding each year comes from the Eckerd Foundation.

Francis of Assisi

St. Francis of Assisi, founder of the Franciscan Order, was born in 1182 in Assisi in Umbria. His father was Pietro Bernardone, a rich cloth merchant. Born into Italian wealth, he found joy solely in seeking after God. Desiring to live a life of devotion without the hindrances of money, he gave it all away and spent his life befriending the poor and sick.

Selina Hastings

Countess of Huntington, born in 1707 of noble birth, Selina Hastings was a English religious leader and founder of a sect of Calvinistic Methodists. During her adult life she worked closely with John Wesley and George Whitefield in the great revival. Using her wealth she built 64 chapels in different areas of England and Wales including Bath, Brighton and London. She converted a mansion in South Wales into a theological seminary for young ministers.

Albert Hyde

Born in 1848, Albert Hyde became a banking clerk for several years. After that he devoted his time to the booming real estate market. When that bubble burst, he entered into a business partnership and created the Yucca Company which later became the Mentholatum Company. This company manufactured and sold toilet soap. Its success depended heavily upon doctors, chemists, good salesmanship, word-of-mouth, and the favor of the druggists.

In search of new products to produce, and intrigues with the properties of menthol, Hyde developed a product know today as Mentholatum, know to cure many ills. The name of Mentholatum came to be linked solely with that of A. Hyde. Other products included fly paper, cough syrup and silver polish.

Becoming a man of great wealth because of its success, Albert Hyde decided to give all of his money away during his lifetime. He gave multiplied millions to the Y.M.C.A. At one time all of his Japan profits from his products was used to support missionary work there. When he died he had given millions to missions. At the time of his death in 1935 he died without accumulated wealth, thus fulfilling his lifetime wish.

Robert A. Laidlaw

Born in 1885 in Scotland, Robert Laidlaw became one of New Zealand's most successful businessmen. He was a self-made millionaire who's first business venture was a mail order company named Laidlaw Leeds. This business was consolidated with the Farmers Union Trading Company in 1918. In 1919 he bought his first 12-store chain and by 1933 there were some 60 branches; business was booming.

Early in his business life he began giving ten percent of his income. He started tithing at the age of eighteen on his weekly salary of just $3. This 10% soon went to 15%, then to 20% and later to 25%. At the age of twenty-five he wrote in his journal, "I have decided to change my earlier graduated scale, and start now giving fifty percent of all my earnings." For the next sixty years he did just that.

He played a major role in establishing several Christian initiatives in New Zealand. After World War II he retired from the activities of regular business and devoted his time largely to church involvement and Christian missionary work.

Robert G. LeTourneau

Born in 1888 to godly parents, accepting Christ as Savior at age 16, Robert LeTourneau dedicated his business life to God at age 30. He dropped out of school at age fourteen and went to work shoveling sand and dirt at an iron works factory in Portland, Oregon. Working around men of the world, his heart became hardened toward God. Just before Christmas in 1904, the city of Portland had a Gospel crusade and LeTourneau decide to attend. After singing hymns and listening to sermons he didn't feel any conviction leading to a quick response. That concerned him so much that he knew he needed to pray for salvation. After doing so, he became aware of a Divine Presence in his life.

He was a designer and builder of earthmoving equipment. He pioneered the welding of various metals, built huge mobile offshore drilling platforms and brought new technology to the earthmoving and material handling industry. During his lifetime his company designed and built some of the world's most massive machinery including bridge building equipment, drilling rigs, missile launchers and earth movers. He was an internationally recognized industrialist.

In his manufacturing plants he employed three full-time Chaplains. He traveled the world sharing the Gospel with other businesspersons. He established missionary ministries in the countries of Liberia, West Africa, Peru and other South American countries. He and his wife founded LeTourneau University. He took no credit for personal success and wealth, but always gave credit to God; saying often, "I'm just a mechanic that God has blessed…".

For most of his successful life, he lived on ten percent of his income and gave ninety percent to Christian work. "The question", he said, "is not how much of my money I give to God, but rather how much of God's money I keep for myself."

Proverbs 28:27

He who gives to the poor will lack nothing, but he who closes his eyes to them receives many curses.

This is a very strong "in-your-face" verse of Scripture which indicates that if you want to go through life lacking nothing, you had better be giving to the poor. Did you ever wonder what it is really like to be in true poverty? In countries of prosperity, few qualify as poor.

While having an adequate income is necessary to sustain oneself, there is much more to a sense of well-being than having a steady income. The good life without poverty includes belonging to a community, having good health, possessing a sense of inner peace, having the freedom of choice, developing a occupational livelihood, working in a healthy environment and enjoying clean air and pure water.

The World Bank website offers the following quotes from people around the world living in poverty.

> *"Poverty is like living in jail, living under bondage, waiting to be free"* — *Jamaica*

> *"Poverty is lack of freedom, enslaved by crushing daily burden, by depression and fear of what the future will bring."* — *Georgia*

> *"If you want to do something and have no power to do it, it is talauchi (poverty)."* — *Nigeria*

> *"Lack of work worries me. My children were hungry and I told them the rice is cooking, until they fell asleep from hunger."* — *an older man from Bedsa, Egypt.*

> *"A better life for me is to be healthy, peaceful and live in love without hunger. Love is more than anything. Money has no value in the absence of love."* — *a poor older woman in Ethiopia*

"When one is poor, she has no say in public, she feels inferior. She has no food, so there is famine in her house; no clothing, and no progress in her family." — a woman from Uganda

"For a poor person everything is terrible - illness, humiliation, shame. We are cripples; we are afraid of everything; we depend on everyone. No one needs us. We are like garbage that everyone wants to get rid of." — a blind woman from Tiraspol, Moldova

"I repeat that we need water as badly as we need air." — a woman from Tash-Bulak, The Kyrgyz Republic

"Everyday I am afraid of the next" — Russia

"After one poor crop, we need three good harvests to return to normal." — Vietnam

"If you don't have money today, your disease will take you to your grave," — an old woman from Ghana

So how is it with you? Do you feel as though you lack something? Try doing what the Bible says to do….**give to the poor.** If you continue doing so, you will lack absolutely nothing.

When you give first, your own personal needs will be automatically taken care of. After all, giving is the Lord's work. It is Christianity in action. Jesus Christ had something to say about giving to others.

Matthew 25:35-40

"'For I was hungry and you gave me something to eat, I was thirsty and you gave me something to drink, I was a stranger and you invited me in, I needed clothes and you clothed me, I was sick and you looked after me, I was in prison and you came to visit me.' Then the righteous will answer him, 'Lord, when did we see you hungry and feed you, or thirsty and give you something to drink? When did we see you a stranger and invite you in, or needing clothes and clothe you? When did we see you sick or in prison and go to visit you?' The King will reply, 'I tell you the truth, whatever you did for one of the least of these brothers of mine, you did for me.'"

In the verses, Jesus was not just speaking about seasonal giving. Of course, during the holiday season of Thanksgiving and Christmas many of us tend to think more often about giving to others. Some people think of giving only around these holidays.

It is pleasant to give gifts to children and family, but how much more desirable is it to give gifts to someone who cannot return the favor, to someone who is not expecting anything from you? What about your giving the other 11 months of the year? How can you be a giver during that time?

Many scriptures in the Bible talk about giving. They instruct us how to give, when to give, where to give, why we give and what to give. All these verses are not meant to bring us down, point a finger in our face and discourage us. They are there to bring us happiness, merriment and a sense of well being! It is wonderful to be a giver in every sense of the word!

The unhappy people in life are those who keep everything for themselves. They are the discontented ones who are selfish, living life only to please themselves and chase after their own personal wants.

Don't block your path to financial freedom! Start giving to others!

Summary

Enjoying financial security in today's world takes more than simply earning a good living. Some people who have made extraordinary incomes for many years are in terrible financial shape and are not prepared for today, let alone their future.

It is essential to make decisions that will help you manage your resources if you are ever going to be financially secure. Many people make enough money to become wealthy by the world's standards. The problem is not our income, but our spending. Many waste much of their hard-earned money on the small and unimportant things. Don't fall into wasteful patterns of living. Make a decision now to be different, to live differently.

You can get started on the road to financial freedom by putting the following 5 simple keys into practice immediately.

Key 1   Stop Spending on Yourself
Key 2   Control Your Cash
Key 3   Live Below Your Means
Key 4   Save for Your Future
Key 5   Give to Others

You've read the book, now go do the right thing.

Source Material

21 Unbreakable Laws of Success, Max Anders, Thomas Nelson, 1996

A Christian Guide to Prosperity; Fries & Taylor, California: Communications Research, 1984

A Look At Stewardship, Word Aflame Publications, 2001

American Savings Education Council (http://www.asec.org)

Anointed For Business, Ed Silvoso, Regal, 2002

Avoiding Common Financial Mistakes, Ron Blue, Navpress, 1991

Baker Encyclopedia of the Bible; Walter Elwell, Michigan: Baker Book House, 1988

Becoming The Best, Barry Popplewell, England: Gower Publishing Company Limited, 1988

Business Proverbs, Steve Marr, Fleming H. Revell, 2001

Cheapskate Monthly, Mary Hunt

Commentary on the Old Testament; Keil-Delitzsch, Michigan: Eerdmans Publishing, 1986

Crown Financial Ministries, various publications

Customers As Partners, Chip Bell, Texas: Berrett-Koehler Publishers, 1994

Cut Your Bills in Half; Pennsylvania: Rodale Press, Inc., 1989

Debt-Free Living, Larry Burkett, Dimensions, 2001

Die Broke, Stephen M. Pollan & Mark Levine, HarperBusiness, 1997

Double Your Profits, Bob Fifer, Virginia: Lincoln Hall Press, 1993

Eerdmans' Handbook to the Bible, Michigan: William B. Eerdmans Publishing Company, 1987

Eight Steps to Seven Figures, Charles B. Carlson, Double Day, 2000

Everyday Life in Bible Times; Washington DC: National Geographic Society, 1967

Financial Dominion, Norvel Hayes, Harrison House, 1986

Financial Freedom, Larry Burkett, Moody Press, 1991

Financial Freedom, Patrick Clements, VMI Publishers, 2003

Financial Peace, Dave Ramsey, Viking Press, 2003

Financial Self-Defense; Charles Givens, New York: Simon And Schuster, 1990

Flood Stage, Oral Roberts, 1981

Generous Living, Ron Blue, Zondervan, 1997

Get It All Done, Tony and Robbie Fanning, New York:Pennsylvania: Chilton Book, 1979

Getting Out of Debt, Howard Dayton, Tyndale House, 1986

Getting Out of Debt, Mary Stephenson, Fact Sheet 436, University of Maryland Cooperative Extension Service, 1988

Giving and Tithing, Larry Burkett, Moody Press, 1991

God's Plan For Giving, John MacArthur, Jr., Moody Press, 1985

God's Will is Prosperity, Gloria Copeland, Harrison House, 1978

Great People of the Bible and How They Lived; New York: Reader's Digest, 1974

How Others Can Help You Get Out of Debt; Esther M. Maddux, Circular 759-3,

How To Make A Business Plan That Works, Henderson, North Island Sound Limited, 1989

How To Manage Your Money, Larry Burkett, Moody Press, 1999

How to Personally Profit From the Laws of Success, Sterling Sill, NIFP, Inc., 1978

How to Plan for Your Retirement; New York: Corrigan & Kaufman, Longmeadow Press, 1985

Is God Your Source?, Oral Roberts, 1992

It's Not Luck, Eliyahu Goldratt, Great Barrington, MA: The North River Press, 1994

Jesus CEO, Laurie Beth Jones, Hyperion, 1995

John Avanzini Answers Your Questions About Biblical Economics, Harrison House, 1992

Living on Less and Liking It More, Maxine Hancock, Chicago, Illinois: Moody Press, 1976

Making It Happen; Charles Conn, New Jersey: Fleming H. Revell Company, 1981

Master Your Money Or It Will Master You, Arlo E. Moehlenpah, Doing Good Ministries, 1999

Master Your Money; Ron Blue, Tennessee: Thomas Nelson, Inc. 1986

Miracle of Seed Faith, Oral Roberts, 1970

Mississippi State University Extension Service

Money, Possessions, and Eternity, Randy Alcorn, Tyndale House, 2003

More Than Enough, David Ramsey, Penguin Putnam Inc, 2002

Moving the Hand of God, John Avanzini, Harrison House, 1990

Multiplication, Tommy Barnett, Creation House, 1997

NebFacts, Nebraska Cooperative Extension

New York Post

One Up On Wall Street; New York: Peter Lynch, Simon And Schuster, 1989

Personal Finances, Larry Burkett, Moody Press, 1991

Portable MBA in Finance and Accounting; Livingstone, Canada: John Wiley & Sons, Inc., 1992

Principle-Centered Leadership, Stephen R. Covey, New York: Summit Books, 1991

Principles of Financial Management, Kolb & DeMong, Texas: Business Publications, Inc., 1988

Rapid Debt Reduction Strategies, John Avanzini, HIS Publishing, 1990

Real Wealth, Wade Cook, Arizona: Regency Books, 1985

See You At The Top, Zig Ziglar, Louisianna: Pelican Publishing Company, 1977

Seed-Faith Commentary on the Holy Bible, Oral Roberts, Pinoak Publications, 1975

Sharkproof, Harvey Mackay, New York: HarperCollins Publishers, 1993

Smart Money, Ken and Daria Dolan, New York: Random House, Inc., 1988

Strong's Concordance, Tennessee: Crusade Bible Publishers, Inc.,

Success by Design, Peter Hirsch, Bethany House, 2002

Success is the Quality of your Journey, Jennifer James, New York: Newmarket Press, 1983

Swim with the Sharks Without Being Eaten Alive, Harvey Mackay, William Morrow , 1988

The Almighty and the Dollar; Jim McKeever, Oregon: Omega Publications, 1981

The Challenge, Robert Allen, New York: Simon And Schuster, 1987

The Family Financial Workbook, Larry Burkett, Moody Press, 2002

The Management Methods of Jesus, Bob Briner, Thomas Nelson, 1996

The Millionaire Next Door, Thomas Stanley & William Danko, Pocket Books, 1996

The Money Book for Kids, Nancy Burgeson, Troll Associates,1992

The Money Book for King's Kids; Harold E. Hill, New Jersey: Fleming H. Revell Company, 1984

The Seven Habits of Highly Effective People, Stephen Covey, New York: Simon And Schuster, 1989

The Wealthy Barber, David Chilton, California: Prima Publishing, 1991

Theological Wordbook of the Old Testament, Chicago, Illinois: Moody Press, 1981

Treasury of Courage and Confidence, Norman Vincent Peale, New York: Doubleday & Co., 1970

True Prosperity, Dick Iverson, Bible Temple Publishing, 1993

Trust God For Your Finances, Jack Hartman, Lamplight Publications, 1983

University of Georgia Cooperative Extension Service, 1985

Virginia Cooperative Extension

Webster's Unabridged Dictionary, Dorset & Baber, 1983

What Is an Entrepreneur; David Robinson, MA: Kogan Page Limited, 1990

Word Meanings in the New Testament, Ralph Earle, Michigan: Baker Book House, 1986

Word Pictures in the New Testament; Robertson, Michigan: Baker Book House, 1930

Word Studies in the New Testament; Vincent, New York: Charles Scribner's Sons, 1914

Worth

You Can Be Financially Free, George Fooshee, Jr., 1976, Fleming H. Revell Company.

Your Key to God's Bank, Rex Humbard, 1977

Your Money Counts, Howard, Dayton, Tyndale House, 1997

Your Money Management, MaryAnn Paynter, Circular 1271, University of Illinois Cooperative Extension Service, 1987.

Your Money Matters, Malcolm MacGregor, Bethany Fellowship, Inc., 1977

Your Road to Recovery, Oral Roberts, Oliver Nelson, 1986

COMMENTS ON SOURCES

Over the years I have collected bits and pieces of interesting material, written notes on sermons I've heard, jotted down comments on financial articles I've read, and gathered a lot of great information. It is unfortunate that I didn't record the sources of all of these notes in my earlier years. I gratefully extend my appreciation to the many writers, authors, teachers and pastors from whose articles and sermons I have gleaned much insight.

Rich Brott

ONLINE RESOURCES

American Savings Education Council (http://www.asec.org)

Bloomberg.com (http://www.bloomberg.com)

Bureau of the Public Debt Online (http://www.publicdebt.treas.gov)

BusinessWeek (http://www.businessweek.com)

Charles Schwab & Co., Inc. (http://www.schwab.com)

Consumer Federation of America (http://www.consumerfed.org)

Debt Advice.org (http://www.debtadvice.org)

Federal Reserve System (http://www.federalreserve.gov)

Fidelity Investments (http://www.fidelity.com)

Financial Planning Association (http://www.fpanet.org)

Forbes (www.forbes.com)

Fortune Magazine (http://www.fortune.com)

Generous Giving (http://www.generousgiving.org/)

Investing for Your Future (http://www.investing.rutgers.edu)

Kiplinger Magazine (http://www.kiplinger.com/)

Money Magazine (http://money.cnn.com)

MorningStar (http://www.morningstar.com)

MSN Money (http://moneycentral.msn.com)

Muriel Siebert (http://www.siebertnet.com)

National Center on Education and the Economy (http://www.ncee.org)

National Foundation for Credit Counseling (http://www.nfcc.org)

Quicken (http://www.quicken.com)

Smart Money (http://www.smartmoney.com)

Social Security Online (http://www.ssa.gov)

Standard & Poor's (http://www2.standardandpoors.com)

The Dollar Stretcher, Gary Foreman, (http://www.stretcher.com)

The Vanguard Group (http://flagship.vanguard.com)

U.S. Securities and Exchange Commission (http://www.sec.gov)

Yahoo! Finance (http://finance.yahoo.com)

Magazine Resources

Business Week
Consumer Reports
Forbes
Kiplinger's Personal Finance
Money
Smart Money
US News and World Report

NEWSPAPER RESOURCES

Barrons
Investors Business Daily
USA Today
Wall Street Journal
Washington Times

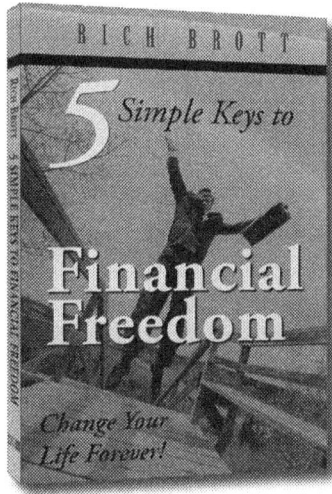

Additional Resources by Rich Brott

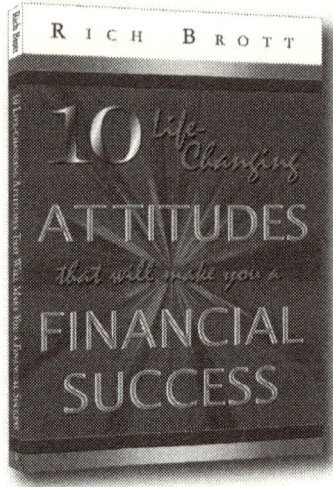

10 Life-Changing Attitudes That Will Make You a Financial Success

By Rich Brott

6" x 9", 108 pages
ISBN 1-60185-021-2
ISBN (EAN) 978-1-60185-021-8

abc
Book Publishing

Order online at:
www.amazon.com
www.barnesandnoble.com
www.booksamillion.com
www.citychristianpublishing.com
www.walmart.com

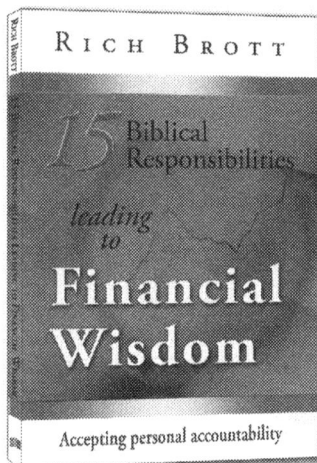

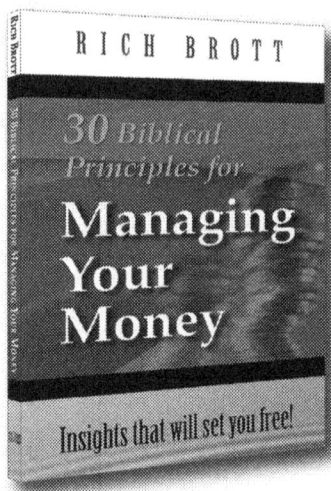

Additional Resources by Rich Brott

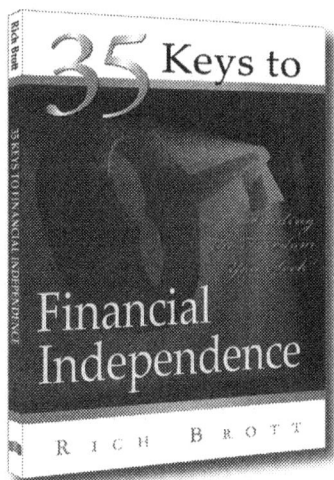

35 Keys to
Financial Independence

Finding the Freedom You Seek!

By Rich Brott

6" x 9", 176 pages
ISBN 1-60185-020-4
ISBN (EAN) 978-1-60185-020-1

a b c
Book Publishing

Order online at:
www.amazon.com
www.barnesandnoble.com
www.booksamillion.com
www.citychristianpublishing.com
www.walmart.com

www.AbcBookPublishing.com

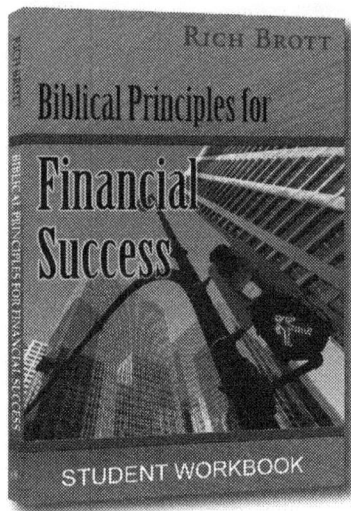

Biblical Principles for
Financial Success

Student Workbook

By Rich Brott

7.5" x 9.25", 228 pages
ISBN 1-60185-016-6
ISBN (EAN) 978-1-60185-016-4

abc
Book Publishing

Order online at:

www.amazon.com
www.barnesandnoble.com
www.booksamillion.com
www.citychristianpublishing.com
www.walmart.com

www.AbcBookPublishing.com

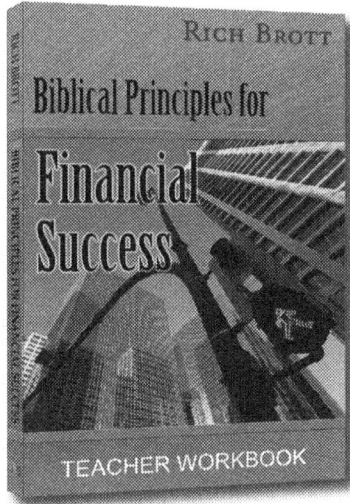

Additional Resources by Rich Brott

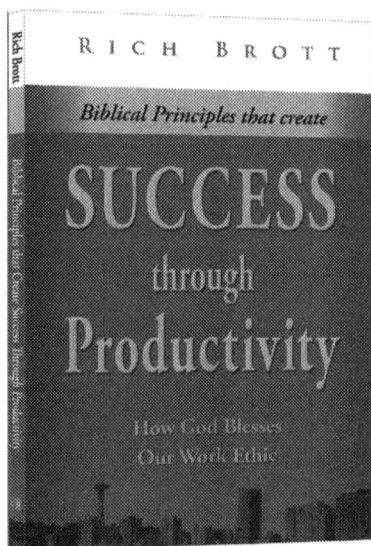

Biblical Principles that Create
Success through Productivity

How God Blesses Our Work Ethic

By Rich Brott

6" x 9", 224 pages
ISBN 1-60185-007-7
ISBN (EAN) 978-1-60185-007-2

abc
Book Publishing

www.AbcBookPublishing.com

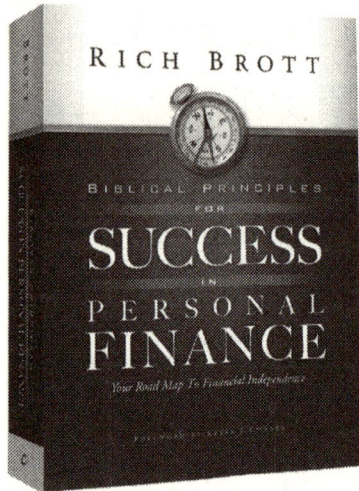

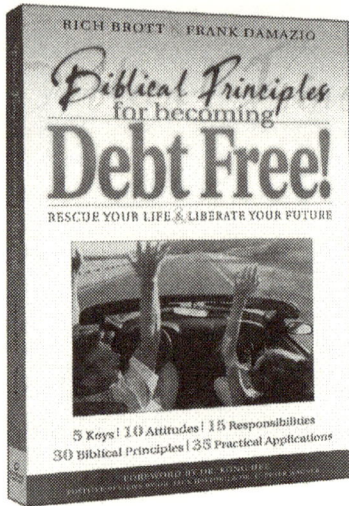

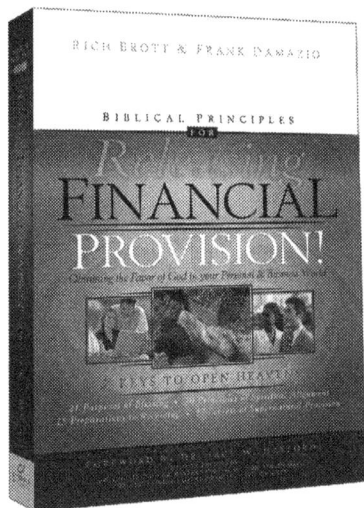

Additional Resources by Rich Brott

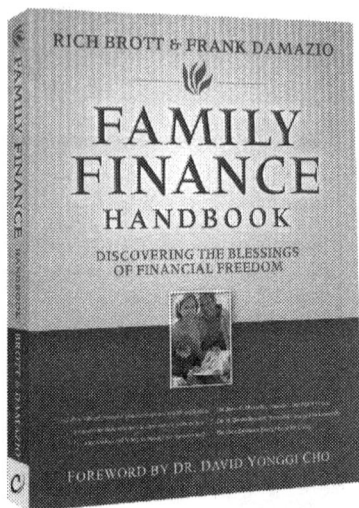

Family Finance Handbook

Discovering the Blessing
of Financial Freedom

By Rich Brott & Frank Damazio

7.5" x 10", 288 pages
ISBN 1-914936-60-3
ISBN 978-1-914936-60-2

abc
Book Publishing

www.AbcBookPublishing.com